A Psychiatrist's Guide

How to Slay
the
Worry Monster!

The Arsenal You Need to Defeat "GAD"!*
*(Generalized Anxiety Disorder)

Martin E. Sodomsky, M.D.

with

Karen Wood

Double M Press   Tucson, Arizona

You may order additional copies of this book or contact the author at: doctoranxiety.com

This edition was prepared for printing by
Ghost River Images
5350 East Fourth Street
Tucson, Arizona 85711
ghostriverimages.com

Printed on acid-free paper

ISBN 1-59975-863-6

Library of Congress Control Number: 2006904934

Printed in the United States of America
First Printing: June, 2006
10 9 8 7 6 5 4 3 2 1

Contents

Acknowledgments

One tenet of the Jewish tradition teaches that a person has to do what he can to save the world. Writing this book is my own attempt to do that. I say this because, as a psychiatrist, I have seen perhaps several thousand patients over the years. However, this book has a chance to reach a much larger audience and convey the message that anxiety and worry is a problem that does not have to be endured and can be treated. As you will note from the book, most people who suffer from excessive worry often do not even know they have a problem and therefore don't seek help for it.

I want to thank my wife, Marilyn, who has offered her help and encouragement to me in the creation of this book. I also would like to thank my children for their support.

To my coauthor, Karen Wood, I would like to give a special thank you. Her writing skills were invaluable and helped me to express technical ideas in a user-friendly manner.

I would also like to acknowledge some of the many psychiatrists and psychologists who have done research in the field of anxiety. These include Aaron Beck, M.D., David Burns, M.D., Martin Antony, Ph.D., David Barlow, Ph.D., Denise Beckfield, Ph.D., Albert Ellis, Ph.D., and Adrian Wells, Ph.D.

I wish to give a special acknowledgment to Karl Menninger, M.D., under whom I trained in the past. Dr. Menninger was the pioneer in humanizing psychiatric care, and it was because of him that millions of people were able to overcome the stigma of mental illness.

Most importantly, I would like to thank my patients, who are the inspiration for this book.

Introduction
How to Slay the Worry Monster

Are you a worrier? Do you wake up in the morning with a sense of dread, fretting about your workload, your upcoming projects, your children's health, your commute into work? Do problems shadow your day, lurking around every corner and refusing to let you relax? Do you even wake up at night obsessing about your problems — how will you meet that deadline, what if the supplies don't come in on time, what if your proposal isn't funded, what if you lose that account?

And along with a permanently furrowed brow, are you tired much of the time? Do you tend to be tense, irritable, and plagued by frequent headaches? Does excessive worry interfere with your personal life? Have family members told you that you are often preoccupied? Do they call you high-strung or accuse you of being "wrapped too tight"?

Does that sound like you or someone you know? If so, you have just taken the first step to solving your problem. Just realizing that you have a treatable condition with a name is a big step in overcoming it. What you have is called generalized anxiety disorder (GAD) and it's very common. I like to refer to GAD as the "Worry Monster." If you are tormented by this beast, it is time for you to take up arms and learn how to slay him.

I can help you defeat the Worry Monster. As a psychiatrist specializing in generalized anxiety disorder, I have more than 30 years of experience with this problem. A native of Canada, I now practice in Tucson, Arizona. I received my medical training at the University of Manitoba and served a residency in psychiatry at the Karl Menninger School of Psychiatry & Mental Health Sciences in Topeka, Kansas, which is known for its excellence in the field. I am a past president of the Tucson Psychiatric Society and former medical director of the Anxiety and Phobia Center of Tucson.

Because of my decades of experience in helping others with this problem, I can tell you that when you have conquered your worries, your outlook will improve immeasurably. You will be happier and more at ease, able to enjoy your life without the gloomy internal soundtrack.

So how did I come up with the Worry Monster? Why is it helpful to think of excessive worry in terms of a big, hairy monster? There are a number of reasons. Painting a picture in your mind of something frightening takes you a step closer to seeing it as something you can handle. By giving it form, the issue becomes more manageable and solutions more accessible. Like the scary demons you may remember from childhood, the ones that hid in the closet and were vanquished only by mom or daylight, the Worry Monster is created by your imagination. Because you created him, you can defeat him. The problem of excess worry is not a stalking beast. It is within you and within your control.

This book is about helping you learn strategies to overcome worry. The methods I describe are mainly psychological and they work. In addition, medication is sometimes used to help defeat the Worry Monster. The medications commonly used in treating GAD are discussed in more detail later in the book.

So gather up your resolve and let's turn the tables on the Worry Monster. Together we can banish him and give you a happier, more realistic perspective on life.

Section One
The Worry Monster Problem

1   What Is Generalized Anxiety Disorder?*

Most of us have at least a nodding acquaintance with the Worry Monster. A thoroughly nasty fellow, he causes tremendous pain, unhappiness, and loss of productivity. Think back on any situation marked by worry. If you are a chronic worrier, you won't have to look very hard. In addition to the mental anguish, can you remember the way you felt? You may have been tense, nervous, jumpy, sweaty, and shaky. Your legs may have trembled. All in all, you felt bad, both physically and emotionally. Living under those conditions is like having a perpetual toothache, with your dentist out of town and nobody answering the emergency number.

The Worry Monster is no respecter of age, sex, or social position. He preys on the young and the old, the student, the teacher, the novice electrician, and the accomplished pianist. Being successful is no insurance against excessive worry.

---

* Generalized Anxiety Disorder is a condition defined in The Diagnostic And Statistical Manual of The American Psychiatric Association.

The worried attorney

Donald* is a married man in his mid-40s with a demanding, high-profile career. An attorney specializing in divorce, he worries every day about his practice. He puts on a confident facade, but inside he is filled with self-doubt. A rather shy man, he is afraid of losing clients to more popular colleagues in the firm and he secretly fears he might be fired. Last year, a disgruntled client made a complaint against him to the state bar association, and even though it was thrown out, he worries constantly that this will happen again. His schedule is fast-paced and stressful, with tight deadlines. Whenever a case doesn't go well, he worries about his reputation in the community. What if word gets around that he is incompetent? What if former clients bad-mouth him to their friends?

Because of his insecurities, he can be very irritable with his secretary, scolding her for the smallest mistake. Frankly, he sees her as the messenger of doom: whenever she brings in his mail, he experiences a spasm of anxiety.

Although Donald usually lunches with colleagues in the firm, he generally feels like an outsider and doesn't enjoy his meal. Always on edge, he envies more popular members of the firm. As he watches his quick-witted associate Barry entertain the group with jokes, he wonders why he can't be popular and self-assured.

Evenings bring no relief as he worries about problems which might crop up the next day. As a result of his constant anxiety, Donald suffers from headaches and occasional chest pain. Although a cardiologist assured him that his heart is fine, he thinks about his

* The names in this and subsequent examples are fictional.

father, who recently passed away from a stroke. His father's health had always been good and Donald fears he might suffer a similar fate.

Work is also taking a toll on his family life. His wife Marcella accuses him of being preoccupied (which he is) and neglecting the children. She nags him about drinking too much wine at dinner and accuses him of becoming an alcoholic. Although Donald denies this, he fears she might be right. Shamefully, he recalls that last weekend he drank so much at dinner with friends that he fell asleep during the movie. Before he goes to sleep, Donald worries that he might need the services of a divorce lawyer himself.

Once the worry process starts, it seems to have a life of its own and cannot be stopped. A person who worries to an excessive degree moves from one concern to the next and back again, an endlessly repeating loop of anxiety. Unlike apprehension that prepares you to face a difficult situation, worry is not useful or productive. Fueled by imagination, chronic worry is like having a buzzing cloud of biting insects circling your head.

But isn't it normal to worry? To some extent, yes. Worry is natural and part of being human. Sometimes its byproducts can be useful, such as when you cross the street to avoid danger or plan how to evacuate your house in case of fire. However, excessive worry is another issue altogether. When worry clouds your mind and overwhelms your thoughts, when it affects your health or your sleep, when it costs you friendships, jobs or joy, it is not constructive.

In essence, worry is a "useless" dwelling on the possibility of a problem, on the chance of something bad happening. Note the word useless, as this distinguishes productive thinking from unfounded fear. The difference between a normal and abnormal state is the extent of the worry, whether it is appropriate, and how much it interferes with your life. If you worry for many hours a day, if you find your worries interfering with your relationships, if you suffer from insomnia, back pain and other tension-related illnesses, if worry interferes with enjoying your weekends and vacations, then you suffer from excessive worry. This is a problem to be taken seriously. There is a high rate of suicide in people who worry a lot. When life is merely a series of unpleasant prospects, it is easy to sink into despair.

Is this you? You worry about things that don't concern most people. It is hard for you to relax. Your worry rarely results in productive solutions. You think that if you *don't* worry, something bad will happen. You worry when things are going well.

So exactly what is the difference between normal worry and excessive worry? Is your tendency to agonize over decisions a footprint of the Worry Monster? Is calling your wife at work three times a day a symptom of excessive worry or just an affectionate husband checking in? The following questions will give you a better idea if you have GAD.*

1. Have you been bothered by excessive worry for more than six months?
2. Do you worry about a number of problems related to work, family, school, or health?
3. Do you believe your worry is uncontrollable?
4. Are you bothered by at least three of the following?

* For a definitive diagnosis, consult a mental health professional.

- Insomnia
- Restlessness (feeling keyed up or on edge)
- Tiredness or fatigue
- Muscle tension
- Irritability
- Difficulty concentrating

If you answered yes to three of these questions, then you may have generalized anxiety disorder.

Much chronic worry takes the form of "what-if" thoughts. What-ifs often lead to cascades of negative speculation and bouts of tail-chasing worry. Read the following lists of common worries and see if you recognize yourself.

IF YOU ARE A PARENT:

What if my child gets sick?
What if my children fail at school?
What if my child gets into an accident?
What if my child doesn't make friends?

IF YOU ARE A BREADWINNER:

What if I lose my job?
What if my boss gets mad at me?
What if I don't get a raise?
What if I can't pay the mortgage?

IF YOU ARE A SPOUSE OR PARTNER:

What if my spouse or partner leaves me or has an affair?
What if my husband gets sick and dies?
What if my partner loses his or her job?
What if my wife gets tired of me?

IF YOU ARE A CHILD:

What if my parents don't love me?

What if we have to move?

What if my parents die?

What if no one likes me?

IF YOU ARE A STUDENT:

What if I fail the exam?

What if my teacher gets mad at me?

What if I don't have time to do my homework?

What if I can't make friends?

IF YOU ARE A SENIOR CITIZEN:

What if I have a stroke or a heart attack?

What if my pension won't meet my expenses?

What if my family ignores me?

What if my driver's license gets taken away from me?

The worried mother

Linda gets up each morning dreading the day. A master of the what-if scenario, she begins worrying about the most precious and vulnerable aspect of her life: her daughters. Is her youngest coming down with the flu? Is the older girl making friends at school? What kind of safety record does the school bus driver have? Should she voice her concerns to the principal? What if there is an accident? Often she calls the school to make sure her daughters arrived safely and on time.

To further monitor her daughters' education, she has worked her way into a position as president of the school PTA. However, she feels that she is not a natural leader and doesn't delegate authority well. Is she too forceful? Did she handle that last meeting diplomatically? Should she try to improve her support among the other parents? Absorbed with these thoughts, she drives to work, too preoccupied to notice that she is weaving in and out of traffic. Linda supplements the family income by working part-time for an accountant, but her boss is a distant and gruff manager and she gets no positive feedback. Business is slow and she fears she will be laid off and not be able to afford braces for the youngest girl or payments for their second car. Always in the back of her mind is concern about her husband's health. He has gained a lot of weight and diabetes runs in his family. How would she manage without him?

After lunch, she begins to fret about the children — have they gotten home okay; will they eat the healthy snack she left or open up a bag of chips; will they watch television instead of doing their homework? What if they forget to lock the door? Perhaps they are too young to be left alone in an empty house. What kind of mother is she?

As on most days, Linda's worries leave her with a throbbing headache. Her stomach is tied up in knots and she picks at her dinner. When the phone rings, she jumps. Unable to relax, she sleeps restlessly and gets up frequently in the night. She wakes up tired, dreading another day.

As I mentioned earlier, worrying can cause both mental pain and physical symptoms. If the Worry Monster has a hold on you, you might notice one or several of the following symptoms:

Headaches

Muscle tension
Fatigue
Irritability
Dizziness
Shortness of breath
Palpitations and chest pain
Diarrhea
Sweating
Difficulty swallowing
Dry mouth
Loss of appetite
Difficulty falling asleep or insomnia
Frequent urination

(Be sure to check with a physician to rule out
any physical causes of these symptoms)

These symptoms are not only distressing, but they add to your already hefty worry burden. In addition to your general what-ifs, you now have health-related what-ifs. What if I have cancer, what if my insurance won't cover it, what if my children grow up without a mother? You get the idea.

The worried senior

At 78, Amelia obsesses about her health. She has some justification for worrying — she had a heart attack two years ago — but her cardiologist assures her that her risk of another heart attack is minimal. Still, she lives in fear. Amelia checks her blood pressure many times during the day. She doesn't sleep well at night and is tired all day. Amelia is afraid of doing anything strenuous, which cuts out the exer-

cise prescribed by her doctor. Her fear has curtailed her social life — she stopped going to her weekly bridge game, even though she was the group organizer. Her closest friend Beverly used to say that Amelia's shoulder was bigger than other people's because everyone leaned on it. Since her heart attack, however, Amelia has avoided Beverly. Her fear of the outside world has grown stronger. Now she refuses to answer the phone and tells her husband George to take a message. Living with a scared shadow of a wife, George is increasingly concerned about his Amelia's mental health. Last Sunday, she even refused to go to church with him.

Sitting alone in her favorite chair, Amelia broods about her health and calls her doctor frequently for reassurance. A busy man with a thriving practice, he rarely takes her calls, letting his nurse try to calm her. Unable to relax, Amelia lies awake at night, waiting for her heart to stop. Her bedside table is littered with over-the-counter sleeping medication, which she takes every evening. Most nights Amelia tosses and turns for hours. Sometimes she gets up and prowls around the house.

Even visits from the grandchildren cannot rouse Amelia from her gloom. Lately she has stopped driving, afraid she will have a heart attack and injure another driver. In addition to her own preoccupation, Amelia has begun worrying about her husband's health. What would she do if he passed away? Amelia imagines herself in an assisted living facility or a nursing home, spending her days among strangers, tethered to a bed and ignored by the uncaring staff. Whatever the future holds for her, she is sure it will be horrible. In addition to having GAD, she is now suffering from depression.

In much the same way as depression, generalized anxiety disorder is under diagnosed by the medical community. It doesn't help that only 48 percent of GAD sufferers feel their problem warrants a mention during their office visit. This means that over half of those with GAD never tell their doctors about their anxiety. Patients are more inclined to talk about their anxiety to family or friends, not their physician.

And even the 26 percent who bring GAD to their physician's attention may come away with unsatisfactory results. Amelia's physician, for example, wasn't familiar with the disease. He just thought she was a garden-variety hypochondriac. Awareness of the disorder and its symptoms varies widely among the physician population. For example, the first medical professional a GAD sufferer is likely to call — a general practitioner or internist — is much less likely to be familiar with generalized anxiety disorder than a psychiatrist. Only 30 percent of physicians are attuned enough to GAD to look beneath the physical symptoms to discover their emotional roots. In fact, only 18 percent of physicians even consider anxiety when questioning patients about their mental health and even fewer — 16 percent — initiate a conversation about anxiety when patients show persistent physical problems. Even patients who are under a psychiatrist's care often fail to mention their worrying patterns. Ironically, GAD sufferers have more opportunities to be diagnosed because they visit their doctors in higher numbers than their less-worried counterparts.

The numbers show that...

Only 48 percent of patients think their anxiety warrants being brought to their doctor's attention

Only 26 percent of patients discuss anxiety with their physicians

Only 18 percent discuss anxiety with a psychiatrist

Only 18 percent of physicians think about anxiety when questioning patients

Only 16 percent of physicians initiate a conversation about anxiety when patients complain of sleep problems or other persistent physical problems

source: Anxiety Disorders Association of America
online survey of patients and physicians, 2003

The reason for this rush to treatment is that worrying tends to cause both physical and emotional problems that cannot be ignored.

But that's not all. Excessive worrying also causes:

- Procrastination, usually caused by what-if thoughts centered on failure and rejection
- Alcohol and drug abuse, caused by attempts to self-medicate to reduce the mental pain caused by worry
- Irritable bowel syndrome, a chronic and embarrassing condition in which anxiety affects your bowels

- Depression, when worry erodes your self-esteem and coping ability
- Marital conflicts, because the more time you spend worrying, the less time you spend with your spouse, partner, and family
- The worsening of any other disease you might have
- Frequent absences from work or school because of worry

Heard enough? These are the kinds of havoc the Worry Monster can wreak on your life. Although unpleasant, the physical symptoms are not usually serious. They can't kill you or shorten your life. But they can add to what is already a hefty worry burden. The Worry Monster can drain the pleasure from your days. He can make you unsuccessful, unwilling to take chances to advance your career or your personal life. He can even make you physically ill. And he is cunning, creeping up on you when you least expect it. A confirmed Gloomy Gus, he can turn your inner light dark. If the Worry Monster is part of your life, you need to take him seriously. Otherwise, he wins.

The bottom line is that GAD is largely unrecognized by those who suffer from it and the physicians who treat them. Realizing that you have it and alerting your doctor is the first step. The fact that even your doctor may not be familiar with this syndrome doesn't mean that it isn't real and you don't have it. Generalized anxiety disorder may sound innocuous, but it is not. It is very debilitating to those who have it. Read on to find out why the Worry Monster has singled you out as his victim.

2 Why You Are Vulnerable to the Worry Monster

If you're a worrier, your vision of life is clouded with doubt and apprehension. You worry about your dog's teeth, your child's test scores, your overloaded schedule, your upcoming dinner party. In your world, humiliation and failure lurk around every corner. You and the Worry Monster are a pair. What is wrong with you? Whereas your friends' lives seem pleasant, your life is stressful and distressing, like having your finger permanently jammed into an electrical outlet.

So why does the Worry Monster pick on some people and not others? Why, in the face of similar situations, do you react differently from your friends? Why are you overwhelmed with anxiety when your best friend feels only mild concern? Researchers have studied this question and drawn a number of interesting conclusions.

- Generalized anxiety disorder (GAD) is twice as common in women as in men. The Worry Monster is sexist!

- GAD occurs in 3-8 percent of the population. Look closely at your friends, family and acquaintances. It is likely that some of them are buying what the Worry Monster has to sell.
- GAD can occur at almost any age. The Worry Monster has no empathy for the young and no respect for the elderly. The worries may change, but toddlers who sense trouble lurking around every corner are unlikely to quit obsessing over imaginary disasters by the time they hit Social Security age.
- There may be a genetic component to GAD. Your parents, your grandparents, or your Aunt Martha may have had GAD.
- If you have GAD, you are also likely to have other anxiety disorders, such as panic disorder, social anxiety disorder, and different types of phobias. You are also more likely to be depressed and abuse alcohol and drugs.
- Only about one-third of people who suffer from GAD receive treatment. The rest worry their lives away or turn to alcohol and drugs for solace, compounding the problem.
- If untreated, GAD can last for years or even a lifetime.

The studies also found that certain childhood experiences are pivotal in those with GAD. For them, childhood may have been the time when the Worry Monster began to sow the seeds of excessive worry. Most of us look back on our childhood as a happy time, filled with fun, playfulness, and wonder. We felt loved by our parents, safe and protected in their care. In turn, this sense of security and well-being made us feel good about ourselves.

For others, childhood was anything but happy. This is particularly true if you had a dysfunctional parent, especially one who was overly critical. While being criticized is a hurtful experience for adults, it is far more devastating to children. Phrases such as "You can't do anything," or "You are stupid," damage a developing self-image and undermine a child's sense of self-worth. Over time, children who are exposed to constant criticism develop negative beliefs about themselves, beliefs that can psychologically scar them for life. The result is a loss of confidence. From then on, the routine challenges of life loom much larger than they are, making every day a struggle to cope.

"You can do anything you want to," said the mother to her daughter Susan. That was the party line during the heyday of feminism, but it required consistency. The mother sent conflicting messages at other times — "You can't learn to drive a stick shift," and "You won't be able to get into that college." And since negative messages tend to resonate more than positive ones, the words Susan remembered were "you can't." She was afraid to try things, to push herself out into the world. She waited to be invited–sometimes she was, more often she wasn't. People learned they could push her around. Despite her accomplishments, Susan struggled with self-doubt.

Then there are those parents who are distant and uninvolved. If your father ignored you during your childhood, it would not be surprising if you concluded that you were either bad or unworthy of love. Again, this situation can result in feelings of helplessness and inferiority. And as a child grows into adulthood, these feelings do not go away.

Another roadblock to growing up psychologically healthy is having a parent who is smothering and overprotective. If you had this type of parent, you might see the world as a dangerous place. Your days, after all, were filled with warnings: "Be careful," "Don't get sick," "You're going to hurt yourself," and "Be sure to get enough sleep." Overprotective parents who forecast danger make children hyperaware that it exists. Instead of giving their offspring a good start toward an independent, successful life, they actually foster insecurity. As a result, overprotected children don't develop self-confidence.

If you had an overprotective parent, you may not have developed a sense of competency. You may have felt unable to handle life's challenges. Because you were shielded from conflict, you may come to believe that you are incapable of handling stressful situations.

Besides a difficult childhood, other factors leading to excessive worry are a stressful environment or situation. Being mugged on the street, sued by your business partner, or losing your job are all frightening experiences. Developing a serious illness — colon cancer or heart disease — can lead to a feeling of vulnerability. In this case, the negative belief is that you do not have full control of your life and that the world is a very dangerous place.

As a child, Roger was diagnosed with leukemia. He spent his childhood in and out of hospitals, undergoing chemotherapy and later, a bone marrow transplant. His illness, which eventually went into remission, shaped his sense of who he was. Because he endured painful medical treatments at a young age, he grew up with a sense of powerlessness. He saw himself as a victim.

Even though these factors can contribute to a sense of helplessness and inferiority, they are not the only source of excessive worry. Your tendency to think negatively, to underestimate yourself and your abilities, and to magnify your problems make it easier for the Worry Monster to set up housekeeping in your head.

However, you **can** change these things. While some people with GAD take anxiety-reducing medications, there are ways you can reduce worry without them, simply by taking a few steps. Read on and I will tell you how.

3 Psychological Disorders That May Accompany GAD

Lesson one in Worry Monster psychology: the guy hates to work alone. Occasionally he goes solo, but most often he brings along a friend or two. In addition to the Worry Monster, you may be visited by some of the thugs with whom he keeps company: that is, you may have generalized anxiety disorder by itself or you may have GAD along with depression or other anxiety disorders. The Worry Monster is a gregarious fellow.

Bad as it is to have the Worry Monster on your shoulder, his friends are equally loathsome. They cause a variety of other anxiety disorders including:

- Panic disorder, with or without agoraphobia (fear of public places)
- Obsessive-compulsive disorder
- Social anxiety disorder
- Post-traumatic stress disorder
- Specific phobias, such as fear of driving or fear of spiders

So that you can accurately determine whether you are being hassled by the Worry Monster alone or whether he is accompanied by some of his buddies, here is a list of questions you can ask yourself regarding anxiety disorders.

Anxiety disorders

Panic disorder

Panic disorder is aptly named. It can come from out of nowhere, taking you from normalcy to heart-pounding terror in seconds. You can be watching television or driving home from work. Sometimes it begins with a breathless feeling, lasting only a tenth of a second. However, your very sensitive nervous system interprets this as a signal to go into full-fledged panic. That breathless feeling sets off your brain's alarm system, a primitive response that originates in the "fight-or-flight" response that protected your ancestors from predators. Adrenaline floods your body. Your heartbeat quickens, your breath becomes rapid and shallow. It can last one to two minutes and then it is gone. But in the meantime, you may think you're having a heart attack, you're dying, you're going insane. You may end up in the Emergency Room, subjected to a battery of tests, which generally show nothing.

And once you begin having panic attacks, your life changes. Because they are so frightening, you may try to figure out what triggers them and avoid it. Struck while you are driving? You may start taking the bus or begging rides from your husband or co-workers. But scary as they are, panic attacks are treatable. The first step? Read the questions below to see if you are suffering from this condition.

1. A panic attack is an episode of severe anxiety that often comes on unexpectedly. Do you experience the following symptoms?
   - Palpitations
   - Sweating
   - Shakiness
   - Shortness of breath
   - Dizziness
   - Numbness or tingling of the hands or feet

2. Do you spend a lot of time anticipating another attack?

3. When you have a panic attack, do you have any of the following fears?
   - Fear of dying
   - Fear of losing control
   - Fear of going insane
   - Fear of passing out

4. As a result of the panic attacks, do you avoid going out? Do you avoid:
   - Going to the store or to shopping malls?
   - Driving?
   - Going to church or synagogue?
   - Going to work or to classes?

If you answered yes to the first three questions, you may have panic disorder without agoraphobia. If you answered yes to every question, you may have panic disorder with agoraphobia.

Obsessive-compulsive disorder

Do you have little rituals that you can't seem to stop? Do you count to 40 between one bite and the next? Do you wash your hands so often that they are red and chapped? Must your desk be perfectly straight, all your papers and pens aligned perfectly? Do you check that your keys are in your pocket and then do it again and again? Do thoughts of slashing knives intrude into your thoughts at odd times?

Obsessive-compulsive disorder is a grab bag of bizarre thoughts and senseless actions. In severe cases, people with this condition may become hermits, victims of their compulsions. Let's imagine that someone suffering from OCD, as it is commonly called, runs over a bump on the way to work. Afraid that it was a living creature in need of help, he goes back over and over — maybe thirty times — that day to make sure. He even calls hospitals in the vicinity to check on possible accident victims. In another example, a devout churchgoer and former Sunday school teacher thinks about killing her grandchildren. Or a woman leaves the water running as she goes from room to room, washing her hands countless times every day.

Again, OCD is treatable. Read on to see if you fit into this category.

1. Obsessions are recurrent, intrusive, and senseless thoughts. Common obsessions include:
   - Contamination — feeling dirty or exposed to germs
   - Doubting — wondering whether doors and windows are locked
   - Aggression — thoughts of harming someone or being overly responsible for someone else's safety

- Sexual — forbidden sexual thoughts
- Symmetry or exactness — excessive concern that papers and books be in alignment

2. Compulsions are rituals or behaviors that are done to neutralize the obsession. Performing them seems to take away the worry and anxiety you feel when you have the obsession. Common compulsions include:
   - Washing your hands many times a day
   - Checking — repeatedly making sure the door is locked or the stove is turned off
   - Counting rituals

3. Do the obsessions and compulsions occur for more than one hour a day?

4. Do you feel that you have little control over the obsessions or compulsions?

If you answered yes to all of the above, you might qualify for the diagnosis of obsessive-compulsive disorder.

Social anxiety disorder

Social anxiety disorder is the most common anxiety disorder. Are you deathly afraid of speaking in public? Does your heart pound at the thought of contributing to the discussion in a meeting? Do you never send back improperly cooked food because you're intimidated by the waitress? Do you buy things you don't want just to please the sales staff? Do you hate to be the center of attention?

Social anxiety stems from an intense fear of being judged negatively. For those with this disorder, rejection is devastating and long-lasting.

1. Do you avoid many social situations because you experience too much anxiety? These situations might include:
   • Eating in restaurants
   • Attending parties
   • Attending meetings
   • Writing or working while observed by others
   • Returning goods to a store
   • Dating

2. Are you afraid of speaking in public?

If you answered yes to question one but not two, you may have social anxiety disorder, generalized type. If you answered yes to only question two, you may have a social anxiety disorder, public speaking type.

Specific phobias

Do you freak out at the thought of a spider? Would you drive around the block to avoid a snake — even a dead snake — in the middle of the road? Do you have night lights in every room because you're still afraid of the dark? Do you refuse to fly, preferring to drive across country?

Common phobic objects include:
   • Animals (snakes, dogs, cats, rodents, spiders)
   • Heights
   • Blood

- Enclosed spaces
- Darkness

If you answered yes to any of the above, you may be suffering from a specific phobia.

Post-traumatic stress disorder

Soldiers and those living in war zones, accident victims, and people who have witnessed or experienced a violent crime may be haunted by flashbacks for years. Something — a backfiring car, a gunshot, a flare of light, the wail of an ambulance — can trigger a surge of panic. Sometimes the flashbacks don't begin until months or years after the event. Nonetheless, they can be serious, leading to avoidance of certain situations.

1. Have you ever been exposed to a traumatic event?

2. Have you ever experienced or witnessed an event in which you or someone else had their life threatened? After such an event, did you experience any of the following:
   - Nightmares
   - Flashbacks
   - Intrusive memories about the event

3. After the trauma, did you experience any of the following?
   - Hyperarousal or hypervigilance (being easily aroused or extremely careful)

- Startling easily
- Emotional numbing
- Avoidance of anything or any person or place that reminds you of the traumatic event

If you answered yes to questions one, two, or three, you may be suffering from post-traumatic stress disorder.

Depression

Depression is by far the Worry Monster's most trusted — and most dangerous — pal. You often see this guy lurking in the shadows with a gloomy look on his face. Just being near him makes you feel sad. Read the following questions to determine if you are suffering from depression.

Have you ever had the following symptoms?
- Sadness
- Feelings of guilt
- Irritable mood
- Less interest or pleasure in usual activities
- Withdrawal from or avoidance of people
- Finding it hard to do things
- Seeing yourself as worthless
- Trouble concentrating
- Difficulty making decisions
- Suicidal thoughts
- Seeing the future as hopeless
- Significant weight loss
- Change of sleep patterns
- Decreased sexual desire

If you have had five or more of the above symptoms for more than two weeks, you might be depressed.

Medical Disorders

Finally, in order to make the assessment complete, it is important that you see your primary care physician to rule out any medical cause for anxiety. Illnesses that can cause anxiety include:

- Hypothyroidism or hyperthyroidism
- Adrenal gland disorders
- Neurological disorders
- Other medical disorders such as heart or lung disease

In addition, you need to consider whether you are drinking too much coffee or other beverages (such as tea or colas) containing caffeine. These can make some people nervous and jittery. If you are abusing alcohol or drugs, this may also cause or contribute to anxiety.

If your answers to these questions lead you to believe you have GAD, this book should be very helpful. If you have GAD in addition to another anxiety disorder, such as obsessive hand-washing or fear of heights, you should visit a mental health professional for treatment. This is particularly true if you suffer from depression, in which case I urge you to seek treatment immediately.

Martin E. Sodomsky, M.D.

Section Two
The Weapons

4 Monitor Your Worry Problems

Now that you understand how the Worry Monster operates, you are ready to begin formulating a plan of attack. Because you cannot see him, you don't know how threatening he is to your peace of mind. We're about to change that.

An important first step in banishing the Worry Monster is to track him, as you would any dangerous foe. By doing this, you will get a good idea of the extent to which he is affecting your life. Currently, you may have a vague sense that your worrying is a problem, but you need a more complete picture. You need to know how much time you worry each day, what kinds of things you worry about and which words or actions are likely to trigger a worry episode.

To be most effective, set a goal to track the Worry Monster every day for the next month. This should be enough time for you to get a feel for how the Worry Monster operates and a sense of the types and patterns of your worry episodes. It will help to write down when and where the Worry Monster strikes. By doing this, you will have a visible "worry record," to which you can refer. Ultimately, the worry record will give you a baseline assessment of your anxiety.

On the next page you will see an outline of a form you can use. It is user-friendly and quite simple to fill out. Feel free to copy this form for your own use.

In the first column, write down the date and the day of the week. This will help you determine when you are most prone to worry. For example, are your worry episodes concentrated during the week or on weekends? Do you worry most on Monday and Tuesday or on the days leading up to the weekend? Is your level of worry about the same every day or does it follow some sort of discernible pattern?

In the second column, note the tension level you feel, as mild, moderate or severe.

In the third column, note the symptoms you are having as a result of your worry. These might include restlessness, shortness of breath, sweating, dizziness, difficulty swallowing, fatigue, dry mouth, racing heartbeat, nausea, diarrhea, or irritability.

In the fourth column, note the amount of time you spent worrying.

In the fifth column, note the worries you are having on that particular day. Are they about family issues, work problems, money, health, or relationship difficulties? As you think about what is worrying you, try to be as specific as possible in your description. For example, if you are worried at work, is it about what your boss thinks of you or about an overly competitive coworker?

Worry Record

Date	Tension Level	Symptoms	Time Spent Worrying	Worry Content
	— Mild (0-30%) — Moderate (31-65%) — Severe (66-100%)	— Restlessness — Fatigue — Tension — Insomnia — Irritability — Difficulty Concentrating — Sweating — Dry Mouth — Racing Heart — Nausea and Diarrhea — Other	— Less than 1 hr. — 1-4 Hrs. — 4-12 Hrs.	**Fill in your three top worries** What if ____ What if ____ What if ____ **Area of Worry** — Work — Health — Family — School — Finances — Other

Estelle, a competent woman in her early forties, came to see me a few years ago. She described herself as a very conscientious wife and mother. Running a smooth household, being involved in community volunteer work, and taking care of her two girls were the focus of her life, and she took a lot of pride in how well she accomplished her goals. No matter how successful she looked from the outside, however, Estelle was being stalked by the Worry Monster. "I seem to have this cloud of worry that follows me everywhere," she told me.

After listening to her story and developing a treatment plan, I told Estelle that it was important for her to begin tracking her worries. I explained that keeping a daily worry record would help her identify and eventually combat her worries. An example of her daily worry record is on the next page.

As you will note, the date was Monday, March 3, 2003. Her tension level was 80 percent. Her physical symptoms included tension, restlessness, sweating, and dry mouth. On that particular day, her worry lasted about three hours. The content of her worries were: "What if my children do poorly in school? What if the school bus gets into an accident? What if my husband doesn't get the raise he was hoping for?"

Estelle's Worry Record

Date	Tension Level	Symptoms	Time Spent Worrying	Worry Content
Monday, March 3, 2003	— Mild (0-30%) — Moderate (31-65%) X Severe (66-100%)	X Restlessness — Fatigue X Tension — Insomnia — Irritability — Difficulty Concentrating X Sweating X Dry Mouth X Racing Heart — Nausea and Diarrhea — Other	— Less than 1 hr. X 1-4 Hrs. — 4-12 Hrs.	**Fill in your three top worries** What if the school bus gets into an accident? What if my children do poorly in school? What if my husband doesn't get the raise? **Area of Worry** — Work — Health — Family — School — Finances — Other

In another case, a college student expressed anxiety about his university courses. His worry record is on the next page. The date was Wednesday, April 27, 2005, the day of an oral exam. His tension level was 90 percent. He worried four hours that day, and interestingly enough, he also worried the night before.

His worries were: "What if I fail biology? What if I can't make friends? What will my family think of me if I don't do well on this test?" His worry record is on the next page.

Martin E. Sodomsky, M.D.

College Student's Worry Record

Date	Tension Level	Symptoms	Time Spent Worrying	Worry Content
Wed., April 27, 2005	— Mild (0-30%) — Moderate (31-65%) X Severe (66-100%)	X Restlessness — Fatigue X Tension X Insomnia — Irritability X Difficulty Concentrating — Sweating — Dry Mouth X Racing Heart — Nausea and Diarrhea — Other	— Less than 1 hr. X 1-4 Hrs. — 4-12 Hrs.	**Fill in your three top worries** What if I fail Biology? _____ What if I can't make friends? _____ What if my family changes their opinion of me because I fail the test? **Area of Worry** — Work — Health — Family — School — Finances — Other

As you fill out your own worry records, patterns should emerge. This is the start of learning how to flush the Worry Monster out from the crannies where he hides. Once you begin doing this, you should feel a sense of accomplishment and progress. Tracking him will also help give you an element of control over your situation. Instead of being a passive victim of your anxiety, you will be taking action and moving toward a resolution of your problem.

Monitoring your worries is a very important tool to gain control over them. As you progress through the month, take time to review the record of your worries, your accompanying tension level and your physical symptoms. What are you worried about most? Put it in a broad category: work, school, or home? Do you worry most about money? Do you worry about your health? Is your anxiety related to your reputation or loss of self-esteem? And this is very important - try to recall how many of your worries actually came to pass. If you think back, you will undoubtedly notice something that surprises all hard-core worriers: 99 percent of your worries never came true. Once you realize that, you will be on the way to recovery. The Worry Monster is now on notice.

5 Learn to Relax

The Worry Monster is a multitasking sort of guy. Not satisfied with messing with your head, he also monkeys around with your body. Not only does he cause your thoughts to race, he performs similar mischief on your heart. While in the middle of a what-iffing session, you may notice a number of unpleasant sensations, sort of a worry-go-round. Your heart may beat rapidly, your shoulders may tense up, your chest may feel tight. You may be short of breath and you may begin to sweat. Your hands and feet may feel numb and tingly.

How can you calm yourself down? That's right, you can actually change the way your body feels by practicing specific exercises. As your body quiets down, so will your mind. Conversely, when you are tense, your mind is more likely to return to that continuously repeating worry loop. I'm about to teach you some techniques that you can do anytime, anywhere to short-circuit the Worry Monster. There is a definite payoff to mastering this technique. The first time you actually take yourself from a nervous to a peaceful state is a magical moment.

There are five techniques you need to learn:

1. Muscle relaxation
2. Diaphragm breathing
3. Meditation
4. Visualization
5. Self-talk

Muscle relaxation

When you are tense, you unconsciously contract all of your muscles. Often, your jaw will be tight and you may be grinding your teeth. Your forehead may be furrowed and your head might ache. Your chest might feel tight. You might be breathing rapidly and it might be hard to swallow. You might notice that your shoulders and lower back are tense.

The goal of this exercise is to relax all of your muscles — the looser the better. Set aside a specific time every day to do this relaxation exercise. Because the benefits only last for about twelve hours, it is best to do it twice a day. I recommend doing this exercise on an empty stomach, as a full stomach tends to decrease the amount of relaxation you will experience. A typical schedule might be thirty minutes before breakfast or two hours after breakfast, and, then again, thirty minutes before supper or two hours after supper.

Once you have set aside a time, make it part of your daily routine. If you don't, you will be less likely to do it on a regular basis. Put this relaxation time into your schedule the same way you do for brushing your teeth or taking a shower.

Find a quiet place, such as your bedroom or another quiet area. Do not take phone calls and be sure to let your family know not to interrupt you. Find a comfortable chair and loosen your clothing. You can do this exercise either sitting or lying down, but sitting is preferable. If you lie down, you might fall asleep, and would not get the benefit of the exercise. However, you may use this exercise to help get to sleep at night.

Sit in a chair with both feet flat on the ground. Don't cross your legs. First, close your eyes. This is not mandatory, but it is more pleasant to do the exercise with your eyes closed. Plus, it helps block out distractions and makes it easier to concentrate. Take a deep, relaxing breath. As you let the air out, notice how you begin to feel some relaxation. Now, follow these directions as closely as possible.

1. Focus your attention on your toes. You might want to take your shoes off. Notice how your toes feel and then relax them as much as possible. If you like, you can first tense and then relax your toes.
2. Moving upward, focus your attention on your feet. Let your feet muscles relax. Again, if it is more effective, tense and then relax your feet muscles.
3. Now focus your attention on your ankles. Let your ankles and ankle joints relax deeply.
4. Now focus your attention on your calf muscles. Let them relax deeply. Notice the sensations as they relax.
5. Focus your attention on your knees. Let your knee joints relax. Let all the muscles and ligaments

around your knees relax. Notice the sensations you feel in your knees as they relax.

6. Focus your attention on your thigh muscles and let them relax. Notice any sensations you experience as your thigh muscles relax.

7. Now, focus your attention on your hips. Let your hip muscles relax. Let the muscles and ligaments around your hips relax. Notice the sensations that you feel as your hips relax.

8. Focus your attention on your lower back. Let your lower back muscles relax. Notice the sensations you feel as your lower back relaxes.

9. Still moving upward, focus your attention on your upper back. Let your upper back muscles relax. Notice the sensations that you feel as your upper back muscles relax.

10. Focus your attention on your chest and your breathing. Let your breathing slow down and become deeper. Notice the sensations you experience as you do this.

11. Moving upward, focus your attention on your neck muscles. Let the muscles become very loose and relaxed. As your neck relaxes, notice the sensations you feel.

12. Now, focus your attention on your shoulder joints. Let your shoulder muscles relax. Notice any sensations you feel as your shoulder muscles relax.

13. Move your attention to your upper arms. Let your upper arm muscles relax. Notice any sensations you feel as they relax.

14. Focus your attention on your elbows. Let the joints and muscles around your elbows relax. Notice any sensations you feel as they relax.

15. Now focus your attention on your lower arms and let them relax. Notice any sensations you feel as your lower arm muscles relax.
16. Move your attention to your wrists. Let your wrists get loose and relaxed. Notice any sensations you feel as your wrists relax.
17. Focus your attention on your hands. Let your hands get loose and relaxed. Notice any sensations you feel as your hands relax.
18. Now, focus your attention on your fingers. Let the muscles in your fingers relax. Notice any sensations you feel as your fingers relax.
19. Focus on your jaws. Let your jaws get loose and relaxed. Let the muscles relax. Notice any sensations you feel as your jaws relax.
20. Focus your attention on your cheeks. Let the muscles in your cheeks relax. Notice any sensations you feel as your cheeks relax.
21. Now, relax your chin. Notice any sensations you feel as your chin relaxes.
22. Focus your attention on your eyes. Let your eyes feel heavy. Notice any sensations you feel as your eyes relax.
23. Focus your attention on your forehead. Let the muscles in your forehead relax. Notice any sensations you feel as your forehead relaxes.
24. Finally, focus your attention on your scalp. Let the muscles in your scalp relax. Notice any sensations you feel as your scalp relaxes.

Now that your whole body is relaxed, just sit there and enjoy the feeling. After a few moments, open your eyes, take a deep breath and release it slowly. You might want to consider recording your own voice reading these instructions in a calm, soothing tone of voice. You may also order a relaxation tape from my website at www.doctoranxiety.com. Use it daily to guide you through this exercise.

Relaxation is one of the most important things you can do to prevent or shorten anxiety episodes. If you are serious about ridding yourself of the Worry Monster, this is the first step.

As with anything new, it takes practice to be fully effective. So if you still feel tense after completing this exercise, don't be discouraged. This is normal: it may take several weeks or longer to achieve a fully relaxed state. Don't put pressure on yourself to relax — that definitely won't work. Just keep practicing and eventually you will notice a significant difference. Being able to will yourself to relax is a supremely useful skill. No longer are you a victim of bad days or unpleasant events. When your blood pressure goes up and you start to become tense, simply put yourself in a relaxed state.

Diaphragm breathing

Let's say that you wake up in the morning and start worrying. Your heart races, you gasp for air, your chest is tight, your muscles are tense. It is only 6 a.m. and you are previewing disaster scenarios, scene by scene.

As your mind creates unpleasant images, your body responds with changes of its own. You breathe too fast, which causes you to exhale too much carbon dioxide, which ultimately affects the blood supply to your brain. The result? You become dizzy and tense. Your hands and feet may go numb.

Conversely, worry can also cause shallow breathing and breathlessness. It is an ineffective way to get oxygen into your lungs, kind of like trying to inflate a tractor tire with a bicycle tire pump. Additionally, shallow breathing only engages the upper part of your chest and you need to breathe with your entire chest, including your diaphragm.

The tendency to breathe too quickly and shallowly can be corrected by slowing down your breathing and using a technique called "diaphragm breathing," also known as "paced breathing," "controlled breathing," or "belly breathing." You may be familiar with this type of breathing from yoga or other relaxation exercises.

This is how to do diaphragm breathing:

1. Sit in a chair with both feet on the ground.
2. Place your left hand on your upper chest.
3. Place your right hand above your belly button.
4. Now close your mouth and begin to slowly breathe in and out through your nose.
5. As you breathe in, try to inflate the lower part of your lungs so that the air in them will push the diaphragm down. Breathe to the count of four.
6. If you do this correctly, your right hand will move outward as you breathe in. If you do this incorrectly, your left hand will move outward.
7. Slowly breathe out to the count of four, and your right hand will move inward.

Don't be discouraged if you don't get it right away. Just focus on pushing your stomach out as you inhale. It will contract naturally as you exhale. It may feel odd at first, because most of us normally inflate the lungs, not the belly, as we breathe in.

An easy way to experience diaphragm breathing is to lie on your back and put a small book on your stomach. Then breathe in, inflating your stomach so that the book moves toward the ceiling.

Another way to see what diaphragm breathing feels like is to lie face down on your bed. Notice how you are breathing, as most people automatically breathe from the diaphragm in that position.

Once you master this technique, use it every time you notice yourself worrying. This by itself will get rid of the physical symptoms associated with worry. Often, focusing on diaphragm breathing will help you forget whatever you are worrying about.

It is also a good idea to do diaphragm breathing throughout the day, even when you are not worrying. Breathing in this fashion will help lower your tension level. Some physicians advise you to diaphragm-breathe all the time, noting that this will help your health in general.

Meditation

Another way to relax is by the daily use of meditation. There are many ways to meditate and the method I favor was developed by Herbert Benson, M.D., a cardiologist at Harvard Medical School.

Sit in a comfortable chair and begin to listen to your breathing. You do not have to change the way you are breathing — just breathe naturally and normally. As you listen to your breathing, notice your exhalations. As you breathe out, think or say the word "one" or any other single-syllable word of your choice. Do this for fifteen to twenty minutes each day. I recommend that you meditate once or twice a day. It seems to work better done on an empty stomach.

After about a minute of this, you might notice random thoughts entering your mind and distracting you from meditation. They might be innocuous thoughts, like wondering what you're going to have for supper, or more worrisome thoughts, like whether your best friend is angry with you for some reason. Whatever they are, try to let them go. Refocus your attention on breathing and repeating the word "one." Sometimes, it is helpful to say, "Oh well," which may help you refocus on meditation. After a lot of practice, you should become very proficient at meditating for longer and longer periods of time.

In addition to enhancing relaxation, daily meditation has been shown to be beneficial in dealing with various medical conditions such as cardiac problems, hypertension, asthma, insomnia and even infertility. I highly recommend meditation as another tool to overcome your worry problem.

Visualization

Another way to relax is to imagine happy, peaceful scenes. How anxious can you be while picturing a spring garden abloom with roses or the red-rock canyons of Utah? Draw on favorite scenes from past vacations. Think about things that make you happy: a sleeping baby, the morning comics, your dog chasing butterflies, a successful golf game. Chronic worriers tend to daydream about the dark side of life: being fired, going bankrupt, getting divorced, dying of lung cancer. Or perhaps your fears are more exotic: being mauled by a bear, falling off a cliff, contracting rabies from a stray dog. The thought of what might happen to you is often more vivid than anything that actually *does* happen to you. Replace those anxiety-generating images with hilltops layered with early-morning fog or sunbeams sparkling on a running stream. What have you got to lose? Besides, replaying old vacations in your head is another way to squeeze a little more pleasure from past good times. Make a habit of doing it every day.

As you imagine these scenes, draw on your memory to draw yourself a mental postcard. Imagine yourself lying on a beach, the warm sun on your bare skin, the smell of your suntan lotion, the crash of the waves on the beach, the gritty feel of the wet sand in your hand. The more vivid and detailed your mental sketch, the more effective it will be. Suit your scene to whatever you feel will be most helpful for the situation. You can choose a calming image, a romantic image, or a snapshot from your childhood.

Some experts recommend visualizing scenes in which you actually cope with the challenge you are facing. Say, for example, you are worried that you might lose your job. Imagine yourself discussing the situation with your boss and conveying your message confidently and effectively. Or imagine yourself being successful: writing an "A" paper, finishing a run, building a deck, or coaxing a smile from a cranky toddler.

Self-talk

Most people — it is not just you — talk to themselves all the time. They don't usually talk to themselves out loud, but some form of interior dialogue is going on much of the time. However, when a person worries excessively, the self-talk is generally negative and discouraging. For example, say that you are worried about your performance on a test. Your thoughts might run along the lines of "I know I flunked that test. Why didn't I study more? Why didn't I anticipate the right questions? I'm probably going to fail the course. I am such a loser."

Sound familiar? Insert your own particular scenario — be it first date, job interview or client presentation. Whatever the specifics, you are programmed by worry to leap to the worst possible outcome — moving from doing poorly on a test to failing the course to being kicked out of school. In terms of assessing the situation, negative thoughts don't help. Moreover, they're unreasonable, overdramatic and rude. In general, people who say these kinds of things to themselves would never talk that way to a friend.

To counteract negative self-talk, it is important first to become aware of it. Once you realize that you are doing it, replace it with reasonable, hopeful self-talk. Don't substitute negative self-talk with overblown, unrealistic thoughts. That's not helpful either. It is important to be logical, objective and constructively critical in all situations. A hopeful, optimistic attitude seems to work best. Many psychological studies show that optimistic people are happier and function more effectively in life. A 2006 medical study in the Netherlands linked optimism to a lower rate of heart attacks. I don't advocate a Pollyanna or overly cheerful attitude, but it is useful to assume that things will eventually work out.

In any event, utilizing this type of helpful, reasonable self-talk will often reduce your anxiety and help you feel better. And watch your tone (as your mother used to say when you sassed her). Not only are the words hurtful, the tone of voice carries its own message. Think about the way that smiling when you talk on the phone gives your words a lift. It's the same thing with the voice inside your head. Try to give it a grin.

The next time you catch yourself worrying, listen to what kind of negative self-talk is looping through your brain and quickly replace it with positive self-talk. At first, it might be a good idea to write out the new self-talk statements on paper. This may help you develop the knack of formulating your thoughts in positive terms. Combine it with relaxation and diaphragm breathing. The more you practice, the more natural this will become.

All of these relaxation methods — muscle relaxation, diaphragm breathing, meditation, self-talk, and visualization — should be practiced whenever you have a spare moment. When you catch the voice inside your head doubting your abilities or disparaging your plans, silence it. If you notice that your shoulders are tense or your jaw is clenched, consciously relax them. If your breathing is shallow, begin diaphragm breathing until you begin to relax. (Again, it is a good idea to breathe that way all the time.) And when the world looks bleak, bring out your mental vacation postcards. Take yourself to Aruba or Tuscany or the Golden Gate Bridge. Gaze out over the Grand Canyon.

In short, pay attention to how your body is feeling. Now that you know how to do it, practice these techniques — alone or in combination — until you have subdued the Worry Monster.

6 Analyze Your Worries

The Worry Monster is a blowhard. You know the type. He thinks he is smart and clever, but if you listen carefully to what he is saying, it doesn't make much sense. You can defeat him with logic. Just stop reacting to him on an emotional level and think it through.

The next time the Worry Monster taunts you, challenge him. Examine what he says and think about what his reasoning might be. Be firm and aggressive. Generally, the Worry Monster does not know what he is talking about. His what-if statements have little substance. This is the chink in his armor and you can defeat him because you have discovered it.

Imagine, for example, that it is a beautiful morning and you snuggle under the covers waiting for the alarm to go off, feeling content with life. You are relaxed and well-rested. Then you begin to think about your day. The Worry Monster whispers into your ear, "What if you lose your job?" Immediately, you start to worry. You begin to imagine the ramifications of being unemployed: the unpaid mortgage and the utility bills, the ballooning credit-card payments. The more you dwell on it, the more anxious you feel. There goes your morning and possibly the rest of your day.

After you learn to challenge the Worry Monster, that scenario will become a distant memory. Here is how to begin. First, keep in mind that the negative thoughts that accompany the worry process are usually illogical and irrational. When examined carefully, they don't stand up to analysis.

So when the Worry Monster raises the specter of unemployment, call upon the lawyer within you to cross-examine him. Your inner defense attorney might say, "What makes you say that the boss might fire me? Where is the evidence? Is it not true that I have a good work record, and that I received a bonus lately and my employer and coworkers like me? Is it not true that I have had this job for many years?"

Most likely, the Worry Monster will have no substantive answers to these questions. His arguments are shallow and lack foundation. The first time you are able to refute his what-ifs, the easier it will be to defeat later arguments.

Another technique is to call upon the scientist within you. Say you have Stephen Hawking or Albert Einstein in your corner. In response to the what-if thought, you would counter by asking for scientific proof. "What is the evidence that I might lose my job?" When he doesn't respond, you say, "These are fallacious arguments and the data do not support the conclusion reached."

Or put a little statistical spin on the argument. Ask the Worry Monster, "What are the odds that I might lose my job?" The Worry Monster rarely has a good answer to that question because he is terrible at that sort of calculation. For example, many people fear plane crashes. Others fear situations that are even less probable. Train yourself to think in terms of the actual odds of something bad happening. Most of the time, you will realize that the probability is very low. This realization in itself can be comforting.

In challenging the Worry Monster, it is important to know exactly what he is saying. Sometimes it is not a what-if comment but some other type of negative phrase. In any event, it is important that you remember the exact wording of the negative thought because that will help you counter it.

In addition to the vague menace of what-if, the Worry Monster has another trick up his sleeve. It's not only what he says, it's the way he says it. He is a master of sneering: using a tone of voice that suggests you are weak, powerless, and not all that bright. "If you did lose your job," he whispers, "you would be helpless to do anything about it. No one would ever hire you again and you would become destitute and homeless." Don't listen to this drivel. In this case, take the bite out of his words by "decatastrophizing." Remind yourself that no matter what bad thing may happen, it is likely that you will be able to deal with it. You have a lot of resources to call upon, your own and those of your family and friends. You have overcome obstacles in the past. So if, heaven forbid, you did lose your job, you would manage. It might be unpleasant, but you could cope. The Worry Monster tries to make you feel that you are untalented and unworthy, and this simply is not true.

Another technique calls for distracting yourself from gloomy speculations. Move from problem to solution. "What can I do about this situation? What plans can I make if I do lose my job? Where can I get advice? How can I cut expenses?" The purpose of these questions is to get you to center your attention on a plan of action and not on feeling helpless.

It is better to think of worry as a series of episodes rather than as one continuous process. Just as the lumberjack does not try to cut down the entire forest with one stroke of his ax, it is more effective to tackle your worries one by one. Don't try to defeat all of your worries at once — you'll just be overwhelmed.

I recommend that you keep track of your worries by writing down the particulars of each worry episode. On the next page there is a form you can use. This form differs from the "Worry Record" in chapter 4 which helps you keep track of how your worry difficulties are affecting you in general. The Individual Worry Episode Analysis focuses on one specific worry, your response to that worry and then redirects you to form an alternative, calmer, more reasonable response. In the first column, write down the specific situation you are worrying about. In the second column, note your tension level and your negative thoughts. In the third column, write down an alternative, more reasonable and calmer response which can replace your negative thoughts.

As you complete these worry episode records, include as much information as possible. Try to be very specific, detailed, and focused. Avoid writing vague statements like "I was worried in the morning." Instead, write exactly what you were worried about even if you don't want to think about it again. Many patients have told me that they weren't worried about anything in particular. However, when pressed, they were able to discuss a specific issue or concern.

Individual Worry Episode Analysis   Date: _____

Situation/worry	Worry Response	Calm/reasonable response
Time of Day: ═══	Tension Level:	Consider the Evidence:
Where You Were: ═══	___Mild (0-30%)	
What You Were Doing: ──	___Moderate (31-65%)	
║	___Severe (66-100%)	
Circumstance that Led to Worry Episode:	What If Thoughts:	Now, Reconsider the Chance of a Bad Outcome:
║║║	║║║	║║║

Nora had been seeing me for quite some time. One afternoon, she began to worry because her daughter, Jessie, was not home on time. Jessie was a very responsible fifth-grader, an exceptional and popular student. Nora knew that she tended to be overprotective, so she made a point of allowing Jessie to walk the three-quarters of a mile home from school. On this particular day, it was forty-five minutes after the closing bell, and Nora began to feel a familiar gnawing sense of worry. However, she remembered what I had told her about writing down her worry episodes, and so she went to her desk, got out the form and filled it out, trying to be as specific as possible. You can see her chart on the next page. Nora had already begun to calm down when she heard Jessie opening the front door.

Individual Worry Episode Analysis		Date: Wednesday 4/28/06
Situation/worry	**Worry Response**	**Calm/reasonable response**
Time of Day: 3:15 p.m.	Tension Level:	Consider the Evidence:
Where You Were: In the kitchen	____Mild (0-30%)	Jessie is very responsible. She usually walks home with a group of friends.
What You Were Doing: Making PB&J sandwiches for Jessie's snack	____Moderate (31-65%)	Sometimes she stays a few minutes after the bell to talk to her teacher.
Circumstance that Led to Worry Episode:	_X_ Severe (66-100%)	
	What If Thoughts:	Now, Reconsider the Chance of a Bad Outcome:
Jessie is late coming home from school	What if Jessie was hit by a car? What if she was kidnapped?	Chance of a bad outcome is small.

Even psychiatrists can fall prey to the Worry Monster. Dr. Miller's patient, Sonia, was depressed and pregnant. Her husband was a captain in the Air Force, stationed in the Middle East. Because of her pregnancy, Sonia could not take medication to deal with her depression. When she missed her weekly appointment, Dr. Miller began to worry. Why had he not insisted she take medication despite the slight risk to her baby? Perhaps her loneliness and despondence had become so overwhelming that she had lost all hope and had committed suicide. Being a cognitive behavioral therapist himself, Dr. Miller took out one of the forms he usually gave to his patients and began to fill it out. You can see his chart on the next page. He was able to see his next patients with much less worry. Later in the day, Sonia called to say that she had overslept.

Individual Worry Episode Analysis		Date: Wednesday 5/10/06
Situation/worry	**Worry Response**	**Calm/reasonable response**
Time of Day: 10:20 a.m.	Tension Level:	Consider the Evidence:
Where You Were: In the office	___Mild (0-30%)	Sonia is a very responsible patient. She is looking
What You Were Doing: Reading a journal article on depression	___Moderate (31-65%)	forward to the new baby. She has a network of friends. She
	_X_ Severe (66-100%)	is a very religious person.
Circumstance that Led to Worry Episode:	What If Thoughts:	Now, Reconsider the Chance of a Bad Outcome:
Sonia missed her appointment	What if Sonia committed suicide? What if I missed some warning signs and could have prevented it?	Chance of a bad outcome is small.

You will have taken an important step when you begin to analyze your worries in this way. The minute the Worry Monster sees you reach for that form, he will start to feel himself shrink and his power will drain away. After all, he expects you to sit there and stew in your worries. When you begin to put your worries in perspective, he knows it is the beginning of the end for him.

The bottom line about worries? Most worries are irrational and the vast majority of them never happen. Remember, negative thoughts are usually distorted thoughts. They don't stand up to reasoning or rational analysis. Actually, the odds are much better that something bad will NOT happen. And if it does, you can focus your energies on dealing with it. That's a far better use of your time than useless worrying. It is important to keep up with your worry episode records so that you get in the habit of countering any negative thoughts that crop up. After a while, it will become easy for you to see through the Worry Monster's malicious brand of nonsense.

7 Confront Your Fears

Another strategy you can use to defeat the Worry Monster is to challenge him to a nose-to-nose encounter. Instead of turning your back so he can sneak up on you when your guard is down, turn around and face him. Dare him to hit you as hard as he can. When you don't collapse into a sniveling heap, you've taken the first steps toward victory. Besides letting the Worry Monster know that you're no longer a pushover, it signals a change in leadership. From now on, you'll be better able to deflect his subsequent punches. His strength will wane.

Why does this work? For starters, you won't be avoiding him or distracting yourself from your worries. While a natural impulse, this doesn't do any good because the Worry Monster hasn't left the building. He lives comfortably in the recesses of your mind, waiting to jump out when your defenses are down. So instead of avoiding him, confront him. Try asking the Worry Monster to spell out exactly what he wants you to obsess about. Although he doesn't realize it, asking you to focus is actually counter-productive from his point of view. Why is this true? Generally, people who worry a lot often move from one worry to the next, never resolving any particular issue. You hopscotch from anxiety to anxiety until your mind is buzzing with negative thoughts without a workable solution in sight.

The worried salesman

Joe is a hard-working salesman mired in an economic downturn. He worries about his family, his reputation, and his declining ability to sell washing machines. Joe is bored, frustrated, and terrified. On slow days (of which there are many), he stands around the showroom with the other sales staff, making small talk while trying to conceal his anxiety and growing desperation. Most of his energy goes toward imagining terrible scenarios and unpleasant conclusions. Joe doesn't realize it but there is a simple exercise which would derail his imaginary train to disaster.

Here's how it works. Joe writes down one worry at a time and then imagines each worry in excruciating detail. For example, if Joe has financial worries, he might visualize receiving a phone call from his banker, demanding that he come in to discuss delinquent payments on his Camry. As Joe begins to imagine this nasty message, he notes any unpleasant physical sensations such as tension, sweating, or increased heart rate. Next, Joe imagines the banker coldly threatening to cancel his loan and repossess his car. Moving onto the home front, Joe envisions his wife yelling at him and his subsequent humiliation at not being able to provide for his family. He timidly breaks the news to his teenage children, who will certainly be angry at the prospect of having to beg rides from their friends. Joe thinks about this scene for as long as possible, usually about ten minutes. His anxiety level escalates. Then something surprising happens. Joe gets used to thinking about the worst things that could happen. His initial horror begins to recede and may even disappear.

This exercise is similar to seeing the same horror film night after night. You become desensitized to the knife-wielding freak jumping out of the bushes. Instead of shrieking "NO! Get away!" you think, "Oh, here *he* comes again. Doesn't that knife look fake?" Because you can anticipate the scary parts, they lose the power to shock and disturb.

So when Joe imagines losing his car, he can reassess the probability of this actually happening. Further, he can practice decatastrophizing. For example, as Joe visualizes this scene, he could begin to think about how he might actually handle such a situation. Perhaps if his car is taken away, he could take the bus to work. His children might learn how to deal with adversity by watching their father's example. His wife might get a better-paying job to supplement the family budget. By imagining the worst, Joe has learned that he is much more tough and resilient than he thought. He can adapt to the situation instead of being terrorized by it.

The worried college student

Bill has wanted to be a doctor as long as he can remember. As a young boy, he followed his uncle around in his family practice clinic. In high school, he excelled in biology. Not even dissecting worms or concocting evil-smelling substances in chemistry class dissuaded him from his dream. Now a college

*student, he is majoring in molecular biology to pre-
pare for medical school. His organic chemistry
courses, however, are difficult for him, and he worries about an upcoming test. Despite multiple cram
sessions with his study group, he goes into the exam
feeling uncertain. He worries intermittently over the
next three days. And his worst fears come true: he
fails the test. Bill's anxieties go into free fall. He envisions his entire future at risk, his dreams of becoming a surgeon dashed. So this is how Bill handles it.
He immerses himself in worry. He sits down in a comfortable chair and begins to mentally sketch out all
the horrible things that might happen as a result of
this failure. First, he won't be able to find a decent
job. He'll end up flipping burgers or folding clothes at
a discount store. Okay, maybe not that dire—but anything less than his dream will be a comedown for him.
Everybody will know that he failed—all his friends,
his parents. He imagines the look on his mother's face
as he tells her. He'll be humiliated at parties when
people ask him what he does. He imagines all this,
embellishing and adding to the embarrassing scenarios. He does this for several days and eventually,
he begins to calm down. He thinks of different ways
all of this might play out, how he might react and how
he might look at the situation. Eventually, something
surprising happens. The thought of failure isn't as
frightening as it was. He has faced his worst fears
and moved on.*

As you begin to practice this technique, don't hold back.
Invite the Worry Monster to give you his best shot. When
you come out on the other side of the exercise, you will

notice something remarkable. The balance of power has shifted: you control your anxiety instead of it controlling you.

Although this procedure can be distressing, it is very effective in reducing worry. Combined with the other techniques, you now have powerful antidotes to fight the Worry Monster's poisonous diatribes. When he starts in with his malignant mutterings, you can turn a deaf ear. In the face of opposition, the Worry Monster will wise up and seek an easier target. There is a good reason he took refuge in monster form. He's hoping you won't look beyond the scary face to notice that he is an opportunist and somewhat of a coward.

So, sit down in your favorite chair and invite the Worry Monster to do his worst. Once he sees he can't make you flinch, he will leave you alone.

8 Control and Reduce Worrying

By this time, you probably recognize that the Worry Monster, while a figment of your imagination, is a real problem. However inadvertently, you have rented him space inside your head. As long as he controls how you feel, he's actually got the upper hand in your life. It may be hard to banish the feeling that he decides whether you are going to have a good or a bad day. With him whispering in your ear, you may feel powerless to control your worrying. You may feel that no matter how hard you struggle, those nagging, intrusive thoughts will darken your life.

Actually, you're not at all powerless, you've just been conned. You've got the Worry Monster's number; you just need to let him know that you're on to him. Ultimately, you will prove to yourself (and who else do you need to convince?) that you are NOT controlled by worry. Here's how to do it. Recall those times when you were able to distract yourself from worrying by answering the phone or doing something else compelling. This is evidence that you can control your anxiety and all the other symptoms that go with it.

Here are some additional techniques to help you take back control of your thoughts:

1. **Worry postponement**: Agree to postpone worrying for several minutes. During that time, don't try to forget whatever you are worrying about; simply don't pay attention to it. As you postpone the worry, engage in some other activity such as reading, cooking, gardening, writing, or even humming. Imagine a pleasant scene or happy memory. At the end of two minutes' time, try to postpone the worry for another two minutes. You may be surprised how easy this is. As you become more adept at deferring worry, you will realize that it is possible to control your thoughts. In fact, after a while the worry seems to go away on its own. To be effective, you need to build up your anti-worry muscles, much as you would with any type of exercise. Practice this technique three or four times every day for several days. My patients tell me that they have been able to control their anxiety simply by postponing it.

The worried hypochondriac

Noticing spells of twitching in his legs, George fears he has multiple sclerosis. Because this disease can be devastating and has no cure, he is overwhelmed with anxiety. What if he loses the ability to walk and ends up in a wheelchair? What if the dis-

ease robs him of everything he finds pleasurable? To counteract this worry, he contacts multiple neurologists about his symptoms. He spends $10,000 of his own money for a series of MRIs, CAT scans, and spinal taps. Despite no evidence of MS, he continues to obsess, reading everything he can find on the Internet. Every twitch throws him into a panic. After consulting a psychiatrist, he agrees to a delaying tactic. When a worry surfaces, he postpones it for two to three minutes, then two to three minutes more. So as not to trigger his worries, he agrees not to surf the Internet any more about the disease. After several months, he still worries occasionally, but is no longer consumed with anxiety.

2. **Worry schedule**: With this technique, you agree to set aside a certain time of the day to worry. Set aside, say 5:45 to 6 p.m. each day to worry furiously. For example, follow your worries to a worst-case scenario — your husband dies suddenly, leaving you with huge debts. You must sell the house, move to a bad neighborhood, your car is stolen, your property vandalized, you lose your job, develop cancer, are abandoned by your friends, and die alone and in poverty. Use your own personal agendas, of course. During those fifteen minutes, think along whatever lines your private demons take you. Cram in as many catastrophic thoughts and disasters as you can. Remember, for this technique to work, you have to confine yourself to worrying ONLY during these fifteen minutes. Make a deal with yourself that when you start worrying at other times of the day, you will stop immediately, saving your trou-

bling thoughts for your designated worry time. By doing this every day, you control the worry process. The more you do it, the easier it will be.

Laura worries about her children's welfare at school (are they being bullied, are they learning?) and her husband's health (he has diabetes and heart disease). She puts on a brave face while they are at home, but once they have gone to work and school, she obsesses about these problems. Instead of worrying throughout the day, she decides to schedule a fifteen-minute worry time, slotting it in just as she begins to prepare dinner. During the day, she makes a list of her worries so she can make the most of her allotted time. After doing this for several weeks, she reports to her doctor that although her worries are still with her, she feels more of a sense of control.

3. **Write down the worry**: This is a simple way to interrupt the worry process. By taking pencil and paper in hand, you can control your worry behavior. Be sure to include as much detail as possible — Laura, for example, writes that she is worried that her third-grader hasn't made many friends at her new school and wonders if she should plan a big birthday party this year. What if not very many children come and her daughter is deeply hurt by this? Should she call the mothers beforehand?

4. **Thought stopping**: Another simple way to derail worries is called "thought stopping." You refuse to let worry thoughts into your head or banish them immediately when they appear. Imagine you are in

the middle of a long worry episode and getting more and more upset. Loudly yell out the word "stop" — the louder, the better. This will often jar you out of your worry episode. If you are with other people at the time, visualize a very large stop sign instead. That will provide you with the same relief. Many of my patients find this technique extremely valuable.

As you master these techniques, the Worry Monster's hold on you will loosen. You'll realize that your worry *is* controllable. Once you gain this insight, you will no longer feel so powerless when the Worry Monster comes sneaking in your back door. You'll realize that worrying isn't bringing you success, making you a better person, or keeping you safe. In fact, it isn't doing you any good at all.

9 Focus on the Present

As you know by now, the most effective way to handle fear is to face it head-on. Look it square in the teeth and don't flinch. And while you're within swinging range, examine it carefully from all sides and figure out where its flaws are. If you challenge your negative ideas and stop avoiding fearful situations, something amazing will happen. Your fears will vanish. Not permanently, of course; everyone has fears. But those constant "can't-get-a-handle-on-them" kinds of fears will recede until they become the stuff of memory. Part of the reason this works is that you are taking positive action to combat your fears; you are turning them off, in effect flipping the switch on your anxiety circuit.

However, in addition to everyday fears, chronic worriers tend to have something else in common. You ruminate, or dwell on your fears. And while you are doing that, you don't have time for much else. The outside world goes on without you. Those of you with the permanently furrowed brows tend to focus too much on yourself. You live inside your head (which is why the Worry Monster feels comfortable in there). If you think about it, concentrating on your problems is a fast track to being obsessed with your problems. It is a common trait of people prone to anxiety and depression. The next time you are at a restaurant or party, notice people who seem to be deep in thought and not participating in the social interaction. Once you have recognized it in others, you might find it easier to see it in yourself.

Psychiatrists note that people who focus inwardly are more prone to develop anxiety or depression. Being able to interrupt those interior monologues can help get you into the present, back into the real world instead of the imagined world. And blocking rumination is the best way to short-circuit excessive worrying. Experts recommend that you do it as soon as the worry enters your mind and before the Worry Monster takes the steering wheel.

So how can you learn to do that? What is the best way to direct your thoughts outwardly rather than inwardly? It's fairly simple. Focus your attention on the present, on the here and now. This principle is practiced in yoga and other meditation techniques. By focusing on the present, you not only block out anxious thoughts but more importantly, you begin to notice what is going on around you in the real world. This is a key point, because if you are too preoccupied with your own thoughts, you might not be aware of things around you which could alleviate your worries.

A good example of this is responding to fire in a crowded theater by trying to remember where the exit is instead of actively looking around and finding it. In his book, *The Inner Game of Tennis*, author W. Timothy Gallwey reminds players that to be successful, they need to calm their mind. Stop worrying, obsessing, over-analyzing, wishing, and trying for perfection. Remember the phrase "live in the moment"? That's it. Focus on the ball, its arc, its speed, its color. It is impossible to focus, says Gallwey, if you are consumed with self-doubt. So, just for that moment, lose yourself in playing the game; stop worrying about what you might do wrong, and work on connecting your racquet with the ball.

The worried football player

Todd had always done well in sports; in fact, he played first-string on his high school team. However, when his family moves to a new city, Todd loses his "big-fish-small-pond" advantage. He makes the new team, but mostly sits on the bench. Not being the best player—in fact, being virtually unnoticed—is a new experience for Todd and does not fit with his self-image. He dreads going to practice and his stomach is frequently upset. Game days are Todd's new nemesis. What if he should get pulled off the bench and blow the play? Before each game, he worries himself into a dither, telling himself that he should just quit the team. Todd's psychiatrist suggests that he direct his thoughts away from failure. Instead, he instructs Todd to focus on his physical environment: the sounds of the locker-room banter, the bright lights on the field, the crisp drumming of the marching band, the bustle of the crowd. It sounds simple, but Todd agrees to try. What does he have to lose? Surprisingly, as he pushes his fearful thoughts away and concentrates on his surroundings, Todd begins to relax. By the time the season is over, he has made several important plays. The other players have begun to joke with him and often invite him to parties after the game. Although he still misses his old high school, Todd makes a couple of good friends and sees better times ahead next year. More important than a winning season, however, is his newfound ability to flip the switch on his worries.

So, let's begin your journey into the here and now. Instead of launching your day by worrying about your children, your husband's health or your job, start off your morning by focusing on the mundane sights and sounds of your daily rituals. Let's start as the alarm goes off. You get up, stumble into the bathroom, and wash your face. Take time to notice the temperature of the water, the smell of the soap, the sensation of liquid splashed on your cheeks, the pleasant roughness of the washcloth, the rosy glow of your skin, the slap of aftershave against your face. As you walk out to get the paper, listen to the crunch of gravel under your feet, the crisp feel of the morning chill, and the sunlight glinting off the dew on the grass. At breakfast, notice the texture of the newspaper as you turn the pages, the sweet acidity of your orange juice, the tangy squirt of grapefruit sections in your mouth. Savor the buttery crunch of your toast and the creamy texture of your scrambled eggs. Take time to chuckle at the comics. As you get dressed, notice the texture of your corduroy pants, the silkiness of your blouse, or the geometric pattern of your tie. While you brush your teeth, notice the tang of the toothpaste, the feel of the bristles against your gums, the throat-clearing sharpness of your mouthwash. As you head out the door, concentrate on your surroundings — the weathered hues of your front door, the glow of the brass door knocker, the patterns in the brickwork of the sidewalk, the early-morning trill of the house finches. You're out the door and you have already collected an hour or so of worry-free time.

I have described several different types of distraction — visual, auditory, and sensory. Experts in GAD believe that of the three, auditory is the most effective. Listening to a sound, the fainter the better, can effectively block rumination. The ticking of a wall clock, the hum of the refrigerator, the chirping of a cricket, or the low-pitched rumble of a happy cat all can concentrate your mind and crowd out worries. And auditory distractions are especially useful at night, a time when many people tend to worry.

Here is another exercise you can do several times a day. Set aside about 10 minutes to do this. Make sure you are in a room where you can be alone and uninterrupted.

First, concentrate on the sounds in the room. You might hear the hum of the air conditioning, the tick of the clock or the chirping of the birds outside. Choose your sounds and spend about three minutes listening intently to each one. Let the sound surround and engulf you. Next, choose a color, say red or yellow, and find all the objects in the room of this color. You might choose several red pens or books with red jackets. Concentrate on these items intently and spend about three minutes looking at each one. Appreciate the richness of the color and the variations in hue.

Finally, use the sensation of touch. Feel the texture of the chair in which you are sitting, the clothes you have on, or the pen in your pocket. Feel the surface of three different items, spending about two or three minutes on each one. Notice how it feels to rub your fingers in circles or back and forth. Touch the items lightly, roughly, or quickly.

This technique can be highly effective in increasing your enjoyment of life. It may be difficult at first, but will get easier with practice. As you learn to appreciate these simple pleasures, the rewards will far outweigh the effort.

The point of these exercises is to train your brain to focus outwardly. It is a place you can go anytime you find yourself beginning to worry. The raw materials are available anywhere, in a crowded room, on a bus, in the middle of the night. And the long-term result is that you will be able to resist the tendency to wallow in your worries. If it is helpful, imagine that your head has a switch attached to it, perhaps a chain dangling from one earlobe. You can turn that switch on or off at will. With a flick of the switch, you can turn off the Worry Monster and turn your mind to something pleasurable.

The worried senior

Lorraine, a widow in her seventies, worries about getting Alzheimer's disease. Every memory lapse, every misplaced key, every forgotten name convinces her she is on the slippery slope to dementia. She monitors her behavior constantly and corrects herself unnecessarily. Every time Lorraine forgets a word, she grimaces and exclaims in frustration. She talks about her fears many times a day to family and friends. Even though she has close family nearby, Lorraine worries about what will happen to her if she does develop this horrible disease. Her sister Ellen, after all, is regarded by the family as having lost her marbles. It does no good to tell Ellen anything, because she can't remember it for longer than a minute. What if Lorraine has inherited a predisposition to

Martin E. Sodomsky, M.D.

Alzheimer's? The prospect of losing her mind is too awful to think about. Yet think about it she does. On the advice of her doctor, Lorraine decides to try something different. He suggests that she live in the present, rather than worrying excessively about the future. So she makes an effort to enjoy the little things that make her happy. Every day, she takes time to calm herself by focusing on her physical environment: the soothing rhythms of her favorite Mozart concertos, the sound of the lawnmower outside, the splash of the nearby swimming pool. She turns off her worries to enjoy a rerun of The Lawrence Welk Show, *the spicy aroma of chili simmering on the stove, and the warmth of her down comforter. She enjoys looking through a book of childhood photographs. She plans her next dinner party. She watches the cat snuggle into a nest in the clean, warm laundry. For a while, she chooses not to dwell on an unknown future and concentrates on what gives her pleasure now.*

Focusing on pleasure and on the world around you has another immeasurable benefit. When you do that, you unconsciously gather information that will offset your gloomy outlook, your forecasting of doom. If you cast your thoughts away from yourself, you may notice a friendly smile from a passerby or a way through a difficult situation. If you look at others, you will see reality instead of the projection of your imaginary fears.

The worried speaker

Allen, a high-ranking school administrator, is respected by colleagues for his talent and organizational skills. However, he has one of the most common fears: public speaking. Allen dreads every speaking assignment. He is on the roster for all new employee training sessions and every episode seems to deepen his fear. What if his voice shakes? Is he boring his audience? Will they simply ignore him, or worse, get up and leave? What if his mind goes blank? Allen has reached the point where he is thinking of taking himself off the program, even though it is a good idea for someone in his position to brief new employees. Allen finally decides to seek professional help. At the first session, his psychiatrist tells him about the flipping the switch tactic. Before each speech, he learns to listen to his breathing to calm himself. As he stands in front of the group, Allen takes a moment to really look at his audience. He notices individual faces, pieces of clothing, the hum of conversation. As he begins speaking, Allen watches the audience to see if they are paying attention, talking among themselves, or shuffling through papers. To his surprise, he finds that many of them appear to be taking notes. At the next session with his psychiatrist, Allen is a transformed man. "Doc," he says, "I couldn't believe it. I looked at the group and they were actually listening to me. It made all the difference in the world."

After he learned the technique, Allen found that flipping the switch has all kinds of additional uses. For example, he used to replay each incident in his mind long after he left the stage. As he got further removed from the situation, it was even easier to magnify imaginary gaffes, errors, and badly phrased concepts. At another session, his psychiatrist recommended simply extending the strategy: flipping the *switch on his after-the-fact ruminations. After a few weeks, Allen was able to discard much of the anxiety that had plagued his work life.*

Allen's obsessing over what he might do wrong obscured the true situation. Simply worrying about something has the effect of magnifying it. And fear is often paralyzing. Think about it: If you dread going to work because it is not nearly as enjoyable as reading a book or going to the movies, you tend to forget that there are aspects of your work that are satisfying; the pleasure of accomplishment, the mastery of a difficult task, the praise of your colleagues. Because you — especially you worriers — know that life is not always happy, finding joy in ordinary things can change your whole world view. Try it.

10 Eliminate Worry Behavior

You can also avoid giving the Worry Monster access to your insecurities by changing your behavior. Chronic worriers tend to have certain behavior patterns in common. For example, worriers tend to be perfectionists, and, accordingly, dread making mistakes. As a result, they tend to procrastinate and postpone doing things. They may imperil deadlines by a double whammy: waiting too long to begin a project and then taking too long to complete it by obsessing over every step. In addition, worriers avoid taking on new challenges because they fear they will fail.

Worrying is an example of a feedback loop: you worry and because you worry, you avoid situations, and that triggers more worry. Until you can work up the thrust to get out of that orbit, you are doomed to repeat yourself. What form your worry behavior takes is highly individual. If you worry about having a heart attack, you might stop playing tennis or working in the yard. If you're afraid of having a car accident, you might stop driving. And changing your life because of worry strengthens the pattern and focuses you on the negative. Gradually you will restrict more and more activities until your tombstone eventually reads, "Died at forty, buried at eighty."

Here are some of the behaviors shared by chronic worriers. Procrastination is one of the biggest stumbling blocks and also one of the easiest to work on. For the next month, jot down any activity you have been postponing and force yourself to do it. The less you give in to your procrastination, the weaker the tendency will become. And trust me, doing it will feel so good that you will be less likely to slip back into the procrastination habit. The sense of accomplishment will reinforce your new "do-it-and-get-it-over-with" attitude. That's why making lists and crossing off things is so satisfying. You have done something and you have a record of it.

People who worry tend to drive their families nuts by always asking for reassurance. "Do you think I'm going to lose my job?" "What if the test results are positive?" "What if I didn't mail in the insurance check?" "Am I going to be okay?" This constant quest for reassurance fuels the worry process. Again, you need to interrupt this tendency and resist any impulse to ask for reassurance. Also, if you have a worrier in your family, do not respond to these kinds of questions, as that will only intensify the worry problem.

Often, parents who are worriers use the phone to reassure themselves that disaster has not slipped in the back door while they weren't paying attention. They will call the school to be sure their children are okay or phone their children's friends to check on their safety. Worriers also will call their spouses at home or work for the same reason. This constant phoning and checking is a tendency you need to eliminate. In addition to irritating your family and friends, it actually strengthens the Worry Monster. Plus, it undermines your credibility when there is actually a good reason to be concerned.

Worriers have a tendency to be preoccupied. Because their minds are focused on a variety of what-if scenarios, it is hard to pay attention to what is happening right now. No surprise here: the Worry Monster eats this up — another reason to nip it in the bud. Whenever you notice yourself dwelling on things, force your mind back into the present. You can do this by listening to your breathing or by observing what is around you. In other words, "flip the switch," a technique discussed in chapter 9. Preoccupation can also cause problems in family relationships. If your head is somewhere else, pondering what bad things might be in store for you, it is difficult to spend much time or energy on your family or friends.

Worry takes different forms in everyone. Some worriers are not quietly lost in thought, they are actively preoccupied. They can't seem to be still. Their way of coping with worry is to pace the floor, circle the room, rearrange the shelves, just generally be restless. Think about how dogs "worry" bones. Again, you can counteract this by forcing yourself to sit still and concentrate on the here and now. Stop moving around and listen to your breathing or try the "flip the switch" strategy.

When your mind is full of internally-generated anxiety, trouble coming from the outside may just put you over the edge. Accordingly, some worriers refuse to answer the phone. In the days before telemarketers made dinner-hour calls an exercise in irritation, not answering the phone was more likely to be a way of avoiding potentially bad news. If you don't answer the phone, you don't have to be faced with something unpleasant. Other worriers don't read newspapers for the same reason. If this sounds like you, try the "just do it" strategy. For the next month, answer the phone and read the newspaper. You will undoubtedly find good news mixed in with the bad news. Or screen your calls: listen to the voice mail message. If you keep a record of how many negative calls you actually receive, you may be reassured to realize that most calls were not unpleasant.

It is important to recognize that you can change your behavior to minimize anxiety. If you are doing things to increase worry, you can stop them. Improving the situation is within *your* control. Stop listening to the Worry Monster and take an active role in combating worry behavior patterns. Don't procrastinate, don't constantly ask for reassurance, don't muddle up your head with what-ifs, don't pace the floor, don't avoid bulletins from the outside world. Now that you know so much more about the mechanisms of anxiety, examine your behavior to see if you have other worry-prolonging habits.

11

Use Your Imagination to Turn Off Your Fears

We all know how pervasive media-generated messages can be. Like those annoying ditties (you can insert your own annoying tune here) you'd prefer to forget, they seem to get inside your head and stay there, singing inside your brain in an endless loop. However, if you are like many chronic worriers, your own internal soundtrack is usually gloomy and you can't seem to shut it off. It warns of disaster, it whispers about everything that could go wrong. Sometimes the reason you can't seem to stop generating negative thoughts is that you have been tuning into Worry Monster Television (WMTV). Those scary images are scripted, produced, and directed by the Worry Monster himself. Although his production values are not very high, he is wickedly effective. And there are no commercial interruptions.

What happens when you tune into WMTV? For one thing, his programming doesn't include any sitcoms or game shows. This is daytime drama all the way, plus the Worry Monster's take on reality television (in his reality, everybody gets voted off the island and nobody has the slightest bit of talent). So what does he choose to show you? Hint: he never shows good times; he nixed that congratulatory note from a friend or that image of you sitting at the sidewalk café on the Left Bank. Instead, you get a steady diet of disaster, personalized, of course, to the life the Worry Monster has written for you. You may watch yourself being rejected, dying of lung cancer, or being paralyzed in a car crash. Whatever is most worrisome to you is on the schedule at Worry Monster Television. Your mother will have a stroke, your dog will be poisoned by the neighbors, and your college-age student changes majors four times and will probably never move out of the house. Your toddler is kidnapped in the grocery store. As a fourteen-year-old, you fail chemistry. If you are in the fourth grade, your parents die or take off for the weekend and never return.

Because the Worry Monster has the inside track to your fears, every show will hit home in some way. These productions are usually in color but sometimes they appear in black and white. Either way, they can haunt you for days or even weeks.

The solution to this problem is obvious — turn off the TV or at least turn down the sound and darken the image until you can't see or hear it any more. By taking action, hiding the remote and actually getting up from the couch, you begin to exert some control over the Worry Monster's regularly scheduled programming.

How do you turn off WMTV? It's easy. Just use your imagination. Envision a television. Make it as big as you want. Look at the screen of your imaginary TV. Then visualize yourself walking across the room and punching the "off" button. As the picture fades, so will your worries.

Because you have given form to your fears, because you have imagined an actual television screen instead of a shadowy voice, your worries are no longer part of you. You can deal with them more objectively. If you do a good job at this, your anxiety level will decrease markedly. So today, make a point of not watching WMTV. It always gets bad ratings anyway.

Perhaps you're not a TV watcher. You may prefer radio, which requires that you supply the images to go along with the soundtrack. However, this is no problem for the Worry Monster, who also owns a radio station (WMR). His radio programming is just as gloomy as his TV schedule. All day long, the voice on the radio says things like:

"Watch out!"
"What if you fail?"
"What if you get sick?"
"What if you say something stupid?"
"What if you really are stupid?"
"What if people figure that out and you get fired?"

These comments are actually negative self-talk coming to you through Worry Monster Radio. Again, the solution is simple. Turn off the radio. You own it and you can do it. Imagine a radio set and then imagine yourself walking over and flipping the off switch. When you do that in your mind, you will distance yourself from these negative thoughts.

If you can't turn off the radio, turning down the sound will be just as effective. Or imagine that the radio is far away from you, perhaps in another room. Imagine that the sound is faint and you have to strain to make out the words. Think about it. Do you really want to hear all those gloomy predictions?

One of my teenage patients used her creativity to defang the Worry Monster. In a clever casting decision, she hired Donald Duck as the new announcer on Worry Monster Radio. The former on-air talent was creepily seductive and seemed to know how to tap into her anxieties. Donald Duck, on the other hand, was saying the same things — be afraid of elevators or of going to class — but he was less than convincing as a voice of doom. As a general rule, ducks are not all that threatening and Donald was one of the sillier of his species. Every time she heard him quack his warnings, it made her laugh. She certainly did not take *him* seriously. As a result, she was much calmer and more comfortable.

Another one of my patients, a teacher named Margaret, told me how she used her imagination to combat her worries. She created an imaginary "worry basket." This idea came to her one morning as she was waking up and beginning to face her usual onslaught of worries. Would her students behave when the principal came in to observe her classroom? Would she get a complaint from one of the parents? Would she be able to maintain her composure when the class bully began causing havoc?

How wonderful it would be if she could just throw her worries away with the trash. Margaret imagined a worry wastebasket — one with a lid that could be securely fastened. She visualized herself putting each of her worries, one by one, into the worry wastebasket and closing the lid with a satisfying snap. She was amazed at how much calmer she felt. Margaret realized that she could keep her worries securely confined to her basket as long as she wanted and let them out only when *she* chose to do so. And it was satisfying to imagine the Worry Monster crammed into that wastebasket — limbs entangled, feet up around his ears, his furious cries muffled by his plastic prison.

Using your imagination to create an external place for your worries — be it a television, radio, or wastebasket — is a technique that many people find helpful. In fact, many of my patients say that this method of outsmarting the Worry Monster is more effective than any other. So, take up a new hobby — knitting, reading, gardening, hiking, or cooking — and leave the Worry Monster wondering where he went wrong.

12 Reframe Your Perspective on Worry

By now, you have probably realized that no one views the Worry Monster as a trusted pal. He delights in our pain, he revels in our unhappiness. After all, from his point of view, causing anxiety just means he is doing his job. However, many of us behave as if the Worry Monster has some good qualities. We think that by letting him hang around, we are somehow controlling what happens to us. Ironically, our own actions invite him to stick around, to be more inventive.

How can this be? The most common explanation for this behavior makes a certain kind of sense, even if the logic is a tad leaky. Let's take a closer look at it. On some level, we believe that worrying is helpful or at least a necessary evil. We believe that worrying will prevent bad things from happening or prepare us to take evasive action. It is a throwback to our most primitive brain functioning, our "fight-or-flight" mechanism. Although we aren't often faced with the life-threatening situations that the fight-or-flight response was designed to handle, our body still retains that reaction pattern. We just use it in less critical situations.

Here's an example. Let's say that your boss, who is normally sweet-tempered, gives you a dirty look. At this point, you have two options. You can push it from your mind or you can worry about it. If you are not a confirmed worrier, you might come up with a number of reasons for his sour expression, none of which has anything to do with you or the job you are doing. You might notice his red nose and nasal voice and reason that he might not be feeling well. Or you may remember overhearing that his teen-age son has crashed the family's brand-new Lexus. If you think about it, your boss's scowl could have nothing at all to do with you.

However, if you are a worrier, you're not likely to brush aside even something as potentially benign as a dirty look. What if it is related to something you've done? Perhaps you should analyze the situation so you can minimize any damage to your reputation. You begin to think about all the negative implications the boss's displeasure might have for you and your future. When you do this, you unleash the Worry Monster, now operating (from constant practice) at the top of his game. He turns on the pressure and instantly your mind goes into early panic mode.

If you are a world-class worrier, your thoughts begin to coalesce into the form of specific fears. What does the boss really think of me? What if I get laid off? How will I be able to support my family? A mind riddled with worry does not think clearly. This is why you may actually perceive the very act of worrying as a protective shield. If you don't worry, you aren't paying attention to your surroundings, to potential dangers. It's a form of faulty information processing. The Worry Monster is apt to whisper that worrying can actually ward off dire consequences. Not worrying, he says, can expose you to the surprise of disaster. If you worry, it will not, cannot happen. You will be prepared. Don't listen to this claptrap. As usual, the Worry Monster is wrong. Unless you are worrying about crossing against traffic or planning an escape plan in case your house catches fire, you are not doing anything constructive. Obsessive worry is NOT a helpful overall strategy toward life. It is potentially crippling and deprives you of the pleasure of anticipating good things.

Many people buy into the theory that worrying keeps you on your toes. This, too, is probably an attitude you learned in earlier years. Aside from being inefficient and useless, this attitude is clearly false. Think back on your own experience: how much of what you worried about actually came true? How much time did you spend agonizing and planning worst-case scenarios for events that never came to pass? About 99 percent of what happens to you is of no consequence and certainly no threat to your family. However, if you believe that being hypervigilant is helpful to warding off calamity, much of your life is spent focusing on the negative. Is this how you want to spend your time?

Give some thought to your attitude about worry. If it leads you in that direction, consider the possibility that you believe that worry is actually a friend. This is a very important point. If you view worry as protective or helpful, you automatically worry no matter what happens to you. The good news is that you can break yourself of this habit once you are clearly aware that you have it.

Worry does not protect you

Okay, we've established that excessive worry is in no way helpful. It doesn't protect you, it doesn't make you smarter, it doesn't scare away danger. It isn't the kind of thing you want to invite into your head on a daily basis. Since you probably have already done that, let's establish exactly what kind of foe we're dealing with. The Worry Monster is not the kind of enemy who can cause you serious bodily harm, either mentally or physically. He can aggravate you, make you tense and apprehensive, and interfere with your enjoyment of life. However, he cannot make you crazy and he cannot seriously affect your health. The Worry Monster is more akin to a fly than a wasp. I stress this because some people think that worry can cause insanity or heart problems. The Worry Monster can make you tense and uptight, but that is as far as he can go. You already rent him space in your head; don't feed his ego by giving him more power than he actually has.

The good news is that once people understand worry cannot seriously damage them, the Worry Monster is halfway to the mat. This realization alone can alleviate their worry problem by 90 percent. In fact, psychologists in England believe that these distorted beliefs about worry fuel the entire process. So, spend some time looking closely at what you actually believe about worry—the value, the harm, the consequences. And remember, how much you worry is up to you.

13 Improve Your Sleep Habits

As we have discussed earlier, the Worry Monster is an opportunist. He picks on people who are internally wired to be most receptive to his messages and he also picks his moments. This is why he's apt to show up at night. There you are, lying in bed, waiting for sleep. As the sounds of the day recede and your body settles into relaxation, the Worry Monster begins to whisper in your ear. It starts off as muted background noise, but as the world gets quieter, he turns up the volume. Soon the Worry Monster is narrating the soundtrack to a nightmare. He has interfered with your day and now he is interfering with your night. Think about all the things you have to do tomorrow. What if you forget your briefcase? What if you blow the interview? What if your special order is delayed and you have to deal with an angry client? What if you miss the bus?

Let's digress a minute and talk about the consequences of chronic insomnia. Not sleeping well, as in not getting enough sleep or enough refreshing sleep, is a problem with far-reaching effects. Some studies have linked it to higher blood pressure, and increased risk for depression, coronary problems, and diabetes. Not getting enough sleep can lead to impaired functioning at work or school and more accidents. The bottom line: chronic insomnia significantly lowers one's quality of life.

So how do you banish the Worry Monster and reclaim your sleep? The solution draws upon some of the techniques you have already learned.

First, acknowledge that you are worrying. Don't try to push the worries away. The act of suppression actually prolongs the problem. Accept the fact and try to move on.

Now shift your attention to something else. Let the Worry Monster stay in your bedroom, but don't give him the satisfaction of knowing he is bothering you. He is a bully, so treat him like one. Usually if you ignore bullies, they give up and look around for an easier fight. The Worry Monster is both a bully and lazy, so he is not going to stick around if his target shows the slightest sign of resistance.

To neutralize his mutterings, focus on what is happening right now (similar advice is given in chapter 9). Listen to your breathing, feel the texture of your sheets or the pillow under your head. Listen to the clock or the nighttime sounds in your house or outside your window. Even your husband's snoring can be a way to focus on the here and now, not the dreaded tomorrow.

Another distraction technique involves imagining something pleasant — lying on the beach, hiking in the mountains, watching a brilliant coral sunset. Or distract yourself with insignificant details — think about what you're going to wear tomorrow or what you're going to plant in the garden, something that has neutral connotations. As you focus on these pleasant thoughts, your anxiety level will diminish. Before you know it, you're asleep.

Let me emphasize, however, that you should not try to make yourself fall asleep. This will only keep you awake. Let yourself relax, get into the here and now, and allow yourself to relax into asleep.

In addition to these suggestions, you might find it helpful to follow the "sleep hygiene" recommendations given by experts in the field. Here are some proven techniques to banish insomnia.

- Sleep only when you are tired; if you can't fall asleep within twenty minutes, get up and do something soothing. Don't turn on bright lights, as they will cue your body that it is time to wake up.
- Use your bed only for sleeping or sex.
- Don't exercise for at least four hours before retiring.
- Avoid caffeine, nicotine, and alcohol four hours before bedtime.
- Make sure that your bedroom is dark, quiet, and comfortable. Use a "white noise" machine or earplugs if your bedroom is noisy.
- Eat supper at least four hours before bedtime.
- Develop sleep rituals so that your body is ready for sleep: read something relaxing, drink a cup of hot tea (no caffeine), do relaxation exercises.
- Don't take naps during the day.
- Take a warm bath before bed; after the bath, your body temperature will drop, leaving you relaxed and sleepy.
- Clear your mind of worries; designate a "worry" time earlier in the day if anxiety is keeping you from sleeping.

Practicing these techniques will take you a long way toward blissful slumber. Eventually, you will be able to will yourself into relaxation (always a useful skill) and both you and the Worry Monster will sleep peacefully. Even bullies are harmless when they're snoozing.

14 Boost Your Self-esteem

Sometimes excessive worry is a symptom of low self-esteem. Actually, your worrying may be tied to what *you* think about yourself. Consider the following example.

The worried clerk

John, a young man who had dropped out of college and was working in a hardware store, desperately wanted to find a nice girl to date. His high school experiences had been less than encouraging and he remained scarred by past rejections. Because he worked as a clerk, he felt he was unaccomplished and had nothing to offer women. On a scale of one to ten, he rated himself a two. Before diving into the dating scene, his counselor recommended trying out the wading pool. His assignment was to begin smiling at women he considered attractive. Then, he began to initiate conversations, even something as mundane as asking the girl behind the counter at a fast-food restaurant for extra catsup. He recorded all positive feedback, the data-collecting part of his as-signment. Because requesting more napkins is rela-tively benign, he was able to amass a number of mildly positive interactions with women. After a number of months, he graduated to whole conversations and eventually began dating someone he met at work.

When you're in the middle of obsessing about some-thing, you may not be able to puzzle out the cause of your torment. However, if you poke at it a bit, you may realize that the underlying issue is self-doubt or uncertainty. Down deep, you may not believe in yourself. You may think you are not smart or capable. You may feel worthless or unat-tractive. Follow the belief and you will come right up against the conclusion drawn by your subconscious mind. This is what is driving your worries. You believe that you are no good (in a variety of ways), so it is natural that bad things will happen to you.

For example, if you feel that you are not capable, it is understandable that you would worry about losing your job. If you feel that you are not smart, then of course you worry about failing tests. If you believe that you are not worthwhile, it makes sense that you would fear rejection and failure.

You know where I am going with this. In many ways, you are your own worst enemy. Because you don't believe in yourself, you allow the Worry Monster to echo your own (supposed) inadequacies.

So what can you do about it? First, you need to iden-tify what type of self-doubt you have. Look at the follow-ing list and pick out the negative thoughts that fit you best.

- Intelligence
  I am not that smart.
  Others are smarter.
  I do not have a college education.
- Appearance
  I am unattractive.
  Others are more attractive than I am.
  I am undesirable.
- Self-worth
  I am worthless.
  I don't have what it takes to succeed.
  I'm unlovable.
- Competence
  I'm inadequate.
  I'm a loser.
  I always fail.

Look over these lists carefully. Do you recognize yourself? It is common to identify more than one negative belief. Now let's work on getting rid of those beliefs you carry around. To do this, practice the following steps. They may be hard at first, especially the first one, but they are worth the effort.

1. Ask a trusted friend, co-worker, or relative what he or she thinks of you. Let that person know about your negative beliefs and see whether you can get information to the contrary. Often, others will not only counter your negative views but give you examples that support their opinion.

2. Record all compliments. People often shrug off compliments in the interests of being modest and dismiss or discount them. So write them down. In addition, record all the good things you do each

day. People who don't believe in themselves don't give themselves credit for their accomplishments. Instead, they dwell on all the things they don't do well.

3. Remind yourself that the negative belief is most likely inaccurate. Sometimes people acquire negative beliefs from bad experiences with parents, teachers, or peers. Frequently, as we grow up, we receive negative messages that become labels: you are stupid, ugly, a loser. Insert your own bad childhood memory here. Besides being cruel, these labels are NOT TRUE. In addition to being generalizations, they are illogical. Realize that this harmful evaluation you have about yourself is probably old news. It does not take into account who you are right now, what you have accomplished, and all the things you do well.

4. Read some daily affirmations. Tell yourself often that you are worthwhile. After all, no one is worthless. Affirmations have been shown to be helpful to many people. It is surprising how effective such a small step can be. Reading affirmations — generic phrases designed to boost confidence — can be surprisingly effective. Over time, these canned statements lead to affirmations which are personal to your life. Simply by congratulating yourself for something — no matter how small — or looking for the good in what you do each day, you can gradually change the attitude of the voice inside your head.

5. Treat yourself as a friend, not an adversary. When you make a mistake, take it in stride. Every criticism takes down your self-esteem a notch. Because

you know yourself best, you know exactly how to be most hurtful. Practice patience, compassion, and forgiveness. Compare the way you perceive yourself and the way you perceive others. Don't you normally give them the benefit of the doubt? Would you ever say to them the things you tell yourself every day? Give yourself a break. So you aren't perfect. Who is?

6. Remind yourself of all the boneheaded assumptions made throughout history. People used to think the world was flat until Columbus came along. Taking a bath was considered unhealthy in medieval times. Allowing women on boats is still thought to bring bad luck by old-line lobster fishermen. The same thing can apply to the negative thoughts you have about yourself. You may have had these beliefs a long time, but they are just as false as the idea that the world is shaped like a pancake. The length of time you've clung to these ideas does not mean they are correct.

Once you have more positive beliefs about yourself, you will decrease the self-doubt and uncertainty which rules your daily life. You will be able to relax and worry less. After all, much worry is due to your perception that people are thinking about you in a negative way. Once you believe strongly in yourself, other people's opinion will have less weight. Successful actor John Travolta had parents who instilled such a strong sense of confidence in him that he was generally unfazed by rejection. When an agent or casting director told him to get out of the business, his sense of self-worth was so strong that he thought, "What a silly idea." Comedian Lucille Ball was also advised to forget about an acting career. Even if someone does shoot you down, remember: this is only one person's opinion and it is likely to be wrong.

Even though the exercises in this chapter do not involve the Worry Monster directly, you can bet that the next time he sees you standing confident and smiling, he will turn tail and run.

15   Avoid Being Irritable

Working in the shadows, the Worry Monster is a master at changing your sunny demeanor to something darker. When you shift into a grouchy mood, you are probably also tense. Consequently, your tolerance for even the slightest problem is low, and your tendency to overreact is high. You become angry with others if their behavior does not meet your expectations. Being a continual grouch will not make you popular, and worse, it will certainly damage relationships with family, friends, or colleagues.

So how can you prevent your friends from doing an en masse bailout? First, you need to examine your thought patterns during your fits of irritability. Could the cause of your anger be laid at your own feet?

The unreasonable spouse

Headed out for her weekly bridge game, a wife asks her husband to clean up the kitchen. On bridge nights, this was his job and although he was not as meticulous about cleaning as his wife, he agreed to do it. However, when she came home, exhilarated by good cards and conversation, the plates were still on the table, the dirty pots on the stove. The afterglow of a night of winning hands evaporated in an instant. "You never do anything I ask," she shrieked, and began throwing silverware and slamming drawers. When, still indignant, she told this story to her therapist, he responded that while her annoyance was understandable, rage seemed a bit extreme. Perhaps, absorbed in the football game, her husband simply forgot. Or, when it came to missing the critical play that tied the game, a clean kitchen was definitely a lower priority. Insisting that her priorities be his priorities was unrealistic, said the therapist. In other words, lighten up!

Think about it. When you get angry or irritated at another person is it perhaps because they aren't acting the way you think they should? Are they not living up to your expectations? If so, you are engaging in what psychologists call "should" or "must" thinking. Are you angry because people don't drive fast enough to suit you? You're in a hurry, with only ten minutes to get across town for an important meeting and they're just poking along, blocking your way. How inconsiderate! Substitute any scenario that feels familiar. Does this sound like the way you might react?

Here is what is happening. Because you are irritable, you are being unreasonable. You see a driver ahead of you in the left-turn lane refuse to pull into the intersection and you think, "Why don't they move ahead? They're holding me up and I am in a hurry." When you think and react in terms of "should" or "must," you are projecting your standards and your perspective onto another person. Locked into your own reality, you feel betrayed or violated.

What you are actually doing is demanding that other people behave in a certain way. Does this sound arrogant? If you analyze this situation, you will probably find some element of truth in that. Who put you in charge of deciding how other people should behave, anyway?

In order to change your thinking, you need to ramp down your attitude from "should" to "prefer," as in "I prefer" that people behave in a certain way. Preferring is a much milder sort of mind-set. Instead of blowing your horn and gesturing, you shrug your shoulders in momentary irritation and go about your business. When you switch your attitude, you no longer make a demand on the other person. Instead, you acknowledge the difference between what you want and what is reasonable. Emotionally, you move from toddlerhood to adulthood.

And this is about as far as you can go. You cannot really change what another person does, but you can change how you react to it. Then, when the other person does not behave the way you wish, your anger will most likely be replaced with mild annoyance, which is much easier to tolerate than anger.

This approach was developed by a well-known psychologist, Albert Ellis, Ph.D., who has a number of self-help books to his credit. Dr. Ellis has labeled "should" and "must" thinking as "*must*urbation."

The next time you notice yourself becoming angry with someone, check out whether you are guilty of "*must*urbation" yourself. Switch to the "prefer" mode and see what a difference it makes, both in your mood and your relationships with others. In fact, when you reach the point where you can tell the Worry Monster that you *prefer* he leave you alone, you've taken a giant step.

16 Laugh Off Your Fears

The Worry Monster is a grim creature. Being unhappy himself, he likes to share his gloom with others. However, there is a way that you can distract him from his obsession with misery. Make him laugh: a good joke renders him speechless. And when he laughs, he no longer transmits those what-if thoughts.

Have you noticed that listening to a good joke can make you happy, if only briefly? It changes your attitude, the way you look at things. For a moment, you see the absurd side of life. A skewed perspective can infuse even the glummest situation with humor. In fact, laughter is one of the most effective anti-worry techniques. You may even get so far as to think, "life doesn't have to be scary all the time." It *is* all in the way you look at it.

When I was growing up, my parents used to subscribe to *Reader's Digest*. The magazine ran a column called "Laughter is the Best Medicine." I used to love to read that column and it always improved my mood.

Since laughter is so helpful, I don't know why it is underutilized as a mood-lifter. Being a psychiatrist, I read many journals, and there is rarely a reference to laughter. I think that this is a mistake, as humor can go a long way to relieving both worry and depression.

So how can you use humor in a practical way to relieve anxiety? First of all, remind yourself to assume a lighthearted attitude toward life whenever possible. Although there are certainly serious issues in life, many people behave as though everything is catastrophic. Lighten up! If you look back on it, most of the things that you worried about never came true. Think of all the time you spend unnecessarily mired in unhappiness.

So what can you do to put yourself into a playful attitude? What makes you smile is a personal matter and only you know what that is. Think about it. Perhaps you can start off your day by making faces in the mirror, sticking out your tongue at your family, or telling jokes to your friends. Stockpile books or videos that make you laugh. Read the comics every morning. Watch television shows that you find amusing. Sometimes, it helps to behave like a child, hopping and skipping or dancing around the room. If your family enjoys tickling, that can be helpful.

A good example of the healing effect of laughter can be found in the book, *The Human Heart*, by Norman Cousins. A well-known magazine editor, Cousins contracted a serious illness and used humor to help himself heal. His secret? He watched Marx Brothers movies and *Candid Camera* reruns all day.

Humor does more than just make you feel temporarily happy. There is actually a scientific basis to believing that laughter is a curative. Studies show that when you laugh, the body releases endorphins into the blood stream. These endorphins are natural painkillers and anxiety relievers. And another thing—laughter gives your insides a workout. The act of laughing increases the activity of the diaphragm and improves breathing, which in itself can be refreshing. So try this. The next time you are worried, look in the mirror and make a face. I guarantee this will work. It is hard to be gloomy when you look ridiculous.

One of my patients defanged the Worry Monster by imagining him in infant's clothing. Whatever malignant prophesies he was whispering tended to evaporate when uttered by a tough guy wearing a kitten-patterned bib.

Do you remember the movie *The Wizard of Oz*? There was a scene where Dorothy throws water on the wicked witch and — surprise! — she melts. In the same way, laughter will dissolve the Worry Monster into a heap of nothingness. A fit of giggling literally renders him dumb. So make him laugh. It will improve your mood immeasurably and it will chase the Worry Monster from your life.

17 Exercise Away Your Worries

The Worry Monster does not like to sweat. In fact, he's all but allergic to it. So, in addition to all the other good things it does for you, exercise is a good way to keep the Worry Monster at bay. It won't be effective by itself, but in combination with the other techniques I've outlined in this book, exercise can be a good adjunct treatment.

Why is exercise useful? Theories range from the physical to the emotional and spiritual.

Exercise may work because:

- It helps distract you from your worries
- It increases your fitness level
- It increases certain chemicals in your brain (called endorphins) that make you feel happy
- It increases self-esteem by giving you a sense of achievement
- It releases tension and promotes relaxation
- It helps you sleep

There is scientific evidence to back up the "exercise-makes-you-feel-better" theories. Over the years, a number of studies have been done (including at least three in 2005) exploring a possible link between exercise and improved mood. A study published in the *Journal of Preventive Medicine* found exercising three hours per week as effective as medication or cognitive behavioral therapy in relieving depression. Another in the *British Journal of Sports Medicine* concluded that working up a sweat may be more useful than medication for mild or moderate depression.

Although these studies were directed at depression, not generalized anxiety disorder, it is safe to assume that, to some degree, those results can be applied to GAD. After all, some antidepressants are useful for GAD, as you will read in the next section of the book. And exercise is thought to increase the level of neurotransmitters much as antidepressants do. The more exercise you get, particularly aerobic exercise, and the longer the duration of that exercise, the more endorphins are produced. You will read more about the role of brain chemicals in the next section.

The worried social worker

Right out of college, Jeanne took a job as a social worker. Her job involved finding jobs for people with disabilities. It was a stressful and low-paying position, subject to much oversight by her supervisor. Because they had problems entering the workforce, many of her clients were anxious and — to add to the situation — unrealistic about what type of work they could perform. She had quotas to fill and reports to submit and, this being her first job, her people skills were not that well-developed. She began to take work

*home and to worry increasingly about her perfor-
mance. Because she felt like a failure, her work suf-
fered. To deal with the stress, Jeanne joined a gym
not far from her office. Every day, either at lunch or
after work, she found time to dash over there and
work out. She ran on the track, she joined an aero-
bics class, she worked out on the weight machines.
She made a whole new group of friends. After six
months, she had lost fifteen pounds and could do thirty
push-ups. And because she was more relaxed, she
was more at ease with her clients and more successful in finding jobs for them.*

Although not as good in producing endorphins as aerobic exercise, other forms of activity can also be helpful.
Yoga, for example, can be calming and spiritual. Weight
lifting, stretching, swimming, and conditioning exercises
may help those who have physical limitations that pro-
hibit running or walking.

Whatever exercise you choose, make sure it is something that you like and will continue. The exercise/depres-
sion studies found that exercise was only effective in improving mood when it was something the participants en-
joyed. If you dread your workout, it will just become another thing to worry about. And that will defeat its purpose.

Martin E. Sodomsky, M.D.

Section Three
Medication

Medications Commonly Prescribed for GAD and Insomnia

The human brain is made up of billions of nerve cells called neurons. These neurons form long chains of multiple circuits. Nerve impulses flow along these circuits and regulate body activities. There is a tiny gap between the nerve cells called a synapse. The nerve impulse crosses the gap with the aid of certain chemicals called neurotransmitters. You might think of the gap between nerve cells as a canyon and the neurotransmitters as a bridge that allows messages to cross the canyon.

Why do you, as a worrier, need to know about neurotransmitters? They affect your moods and your responses to events — malfunctions accordingly make you more prone to have exaggerated or inappropriate responses. For example, several circuits in the brain modulate fear. These fear circuits are affected by neurotransmitters, including serotonin, norepinephrine, dopamine and gamma-aminobutyric acid (GABA). There are those who believe that both anxiety and depression are due to deficiencies of the neurotransmitters at the site of the synapse. The antianxiety medications discussed below increase the levels of these neurotransmitters and are helpful for those suffering from excessive fear and worrying.

Antianxiety medications

Selective serotonin reuptake inhibitors (SSRIs)

These medications are prescribed widely for the treatment of anxiety. Although first and most frequently used for treating depression, it was later found that they were extremely effective in combating GAD, social anxiety disorder, and obsessive-compulsive disorder. This group of medicines includes:

Citalopram (Celexa)
Escitalopram (Lexapro)
Fluoxetine (Prozac)
Fluvoxamine (Luvox)
Paroxetine (Paxil)
Sertraline (Zoloft)

These drugs work by enhancing serotonin in the brain. They allow higher levels of serotonin to circulate in the central nervous system, which seems to ease depression and regulate the sleep cycle.

Although these medications have a delayed onset, usually two to four weeks, they are extremely effective for chronic worriers. Numerous studies have shown that they reduce anxiety and avoidant behavior, while increasing self-confidence. In my opinion, the SSRIs are the "Cadillac" of the antianxiety medications. At the present time only Lexapro and Paxil are approved by the FDA for the treatment of GAD.

Compared to the older classes of antidepressants, the side effects of SSRIs are few and most people tolerate them quite well. Major side effects include nausea and diarrhea during the first week of use, but these usually disappear. The side effect most likely to lead patients to stop taking the drug is decreased sexual functioning. There is both a decrease in libido or desire, and a decrease in ability to perform. Sometimes this problem can be alleviated by adding other medications such as bupropion (Wellbutrin).

When discontinuing SSRIs, it is important to taper the dosage very slowly over a period of weeks or months. Otherwise, patients may suffer side effects including dizziness, lightheadedness, and flu-like symptoms.

Serotonin/norepinephrine reuptake inhibitors (SNRIs)

These drugs act on both serotonin and norepinephrine, another neurotransmitter. Two of these drugs are venlafaxine (Effexor) and duloxetine (Cymbalta).

Effexor was first used as an antidepressant, but was later shown to be effective for GAD and is now approved by the FDA for that use. Although its mechanism of action is slightly different, it is equally as effective as Lexapro or Paxil.

Side effects include nausea, dizziness, and sweating, all of which usually subside after a few weeks. Effexor can also cause sexual side effects similar to the SSRIs. Again, when stopping the drug, it must be tapered slowly over weeks or months.

Cymbalta is currently recommended for depression and diabetic neuropathy (nerve pain). Its side effects are similar to Effexor. It has not yet been approved by the FDA for the treatment of GAD.

These prescribed medications and the other medications described in this book can potentially interact with other medications. Accordingly, you should make your physician aware of medications you are already taking. This is particularly important in the case of selective serotonin reuptake inhibitors which can negatively interact with the anticoagulant warfarin (Coumadin).

Benzodiazepines

These medications act by enhancing GABA transmission. This group includes:

Alprazolam (Xanax)
Clonazepam (Klonopin)
Lorazepam (Ativan)
Diazepam (Valium)

Alprazolam, lorazepam, and diazepam are short-acting (less than six hours) while clonazepam is long-acting (twelve hours or more).

Benzodiazepines effectively relieve anxiety. They also have anticonvulsant and muscle-relaxing properties. Klonopin, for example, is commonly prescribed for seizure disorders.

The main advantage of these medications is that they act quickly to relieve anxiety. However, they seem to help the physical manifestations of anxiety — restlessness, sleeplessness, muscle tension — more than the mental symptoms of worry and dread.

Benzodiazepines are widely used. Drowsiness and decreased coordination are their main side effects. Accordingly, one has to be careful driving a car while taking these medications. Drinking alcohol in combination with benzodiazepines is very risky, as the two "potentiate" or intensify the actions of one other. Due to the increased risk of falls while taking benzodiazepines, the elderly should be especially careful.

Despite their effectiveness, there are several major disadvantages to benzodiazepines. They can be highly addicting when taken for any length of time. As with SSRIs or SNRIs, when discontinuing the medication, the dosage must be tapered gradually or severe withdrawal symptoms can occur. Patients coming off benzodiazepines may experience insomnia, anxiety, restlessness, and agitation.

In the treatment of anxiety, it is common to prescribe benzodiazepines and SSRIs or SNRIs together. Benzodiazepines work quickly and most antidepressants take several weeks to become effective. When the antidepressant kicks in, the benzodiazepine can be discontinued.

Buspirone (Buspar)

Buspirone relieves anxiety by enhancing serotonin in the fear circuits of the brain. Its action is very complex.

This medication differs from the benzodiazepine family in that it reaches effectiveness slowly — over a period of two weeks or longer. In addition to being an effective antianxiety medication, it is more useful than the benzodiazepines in easing the psychic manifestations of anxiety. Also, it does not cause muscle relaxation.

The side effects of Buspar are mild, including dizziness, headaches, nausea, and lightheadedness. However, it is not addicting and so can be used on a long-term basis without the risk of dependence. It also has some antidepressant properties.

Tricyclic antidepressants

These medications have been used since the late 1950s for the treatment of depression. They are extremely effective, but their side effects can be a major problem for users. Tricyclics can cause dry mouth, constipation, blurred vision, and sedation. Overdoses may be fatal. In most cases, their use has been replaced by the SSRIs.

One tricyclic, imipramine (Tofranil), is particularly useful in treating anxiety. Although this drug, like all tricyclics, has a number of side effects and usually takes several weeks to become effective, it works well for GAD and is not addicting. However, because of side effects, it is most often used as a last resort.

Miscellaneous

Other medications can be used in the treatment of anxiety. These include:

- Hydroxizine, an antihistamine. Recent studies show that this medication is effective for anxiety, although it can be very sedating.
- Trazodone. An older antidepressant like the tricyclics, it may help curb anxiety. A major drawback is that it tends to be very sedating. It is also used to treat insomnia.
- Monoaminoxidase inhibitors (MAOIs). Another group of older antidepressants, MAOIs are sometimes prescribed for GAD. However, because MAOIs react with foods containing tyramine, patients taking them must follow a special diet. Foods to avoid include aged cheeses, sauerkraut, canned figs, dried meats and fish, and red wine. A recently approved MAOI patch may help eliminate the need

to restrict these foods. Despite the special precautions, MAOI drugs are particularly effective for unusual cases of anxiety.

Insomnia Medication

Many worriers have trouble sleeping. The medications listed below can be used in conjunction with the psychological methods outlined in chapter 13. However, I recommend taking these medications occasionally, not regularly. Using psychological methods and following the steps for sleep hygiene are preferable to taking drugs.

Benzodiazepines
Estazolam (ProSom)
Flurazepam (Dalmane)
Quazepam (Doral)
Temazepam (Restoril)
Triazolam (Halcion)

These medications are effective, but they have side effects including memory difficulties and amnesia. In addition, they can increase the risk of falling, particularly in elderly individuals getting up to go to the bathroom in the middle of the night. Because these medications are metabolized in the liver, they should not be used by anyone with liver disease. Also, there is a potential for abuse.

Non-benzodiazepines/hypnotics
These are a newer group of medications, which also act on the gamma-aminobutyric acid (GABA) receptors. This class of drugs does not have the side effects associ-

ated with the benzodiazepines. Accordingly, they usually do not cause amnesia and there is less risk of a fall when taking them. However, because they are relatively new, there is no available data regarding the consequences of long-term use.

These medications include:

Eszopiclone (Lunesta)
Zaleplon (Sonata)
Zolpidem (Ambien)

Of this class of drugs, Ambien and Lunesta are most often prescribed. They are extremely effective. Because it only stays in the body for a few hours, Sonata is good for people who wake up around 3 a.m. and can't fall back to sleep. This is not the case for Lunesta or Ambien, for which one has to allow eight hours of sleep.

Again, although they are effective, I strongly advise patients not to use these drugs on a long-term basis. They work best when they are only used occasionally.

Melatonin-Receptor Agonist

Ramelteon (Rozerem)

This is one of the newest medications developed for the treatment of insomnia. It acts much differently than the others. Rozerem affects a certain part of the brain called the suprachiasmatic nucleus. This part of the brain controls production of the hormone melatonin, which helps regulate sleep. It is particularly effective for people who have difficulty falling asleep. It is not effective for those who wake up in the middle of the night. Rozerem does not cause prolonged sedation.

Antidepressants

There are two antidepressants that are used "off-label" (not specifically recommended by the manufacturer for this purpose) for insomnia. In addition, they are not FDA approved.

These include:

Mirtazapine (Remeron)
Trazodone (Desyrel)

Both of these medications can help with insomnia, but they have many side effects. In addition to weight gain, mirtazapine may cause prolonged sedation the next day.

Trazodone is widely used by physicians to treat insomnia. It can also cause prolonged sedation and in men, a potentially harmful condition called priapism (in which the penis remains erect for four or more hours without stimulation). In addition, people with heart disease may experience arrhythmia (irregular heart beat) from trazodone and some cases of low blood pressure have been reported.

Over-the-counter agents

For occasional insomnia, there are many medications you can buy over-the-counter (OTC). These usually contain antihistamines; for example, diphenhydramine (Benadryl) is commonly used for this purpose. Although in some cases OTC medications are helpful, there are no long-term studies regarding their safety or effectiveness. In addition, some information suggests that taking them can cause mild daytime sedation. Accordingly, I don't think these are as useful as the medications described above.

While these medicines can help you manage your anxiety disorder, "talking" psychotherapy with a health professional is important to a long-term cure. If you don't address the associated thinking and behavioral issues, including those described in this book, your anxiety will likely return when you stop taking the medication.

Martin E. Sodomsky, M.D.

Section Four
Developing a Battle Plan

How to Organize
Your Plan of Attack

In order to defeat the Worry Monster, it is necessary to have a battle plan. You can't rely on resolve to help keep the Worry Monster at bay. You need a more structured approach: any crack in your armor and he will worm his way back in.

To help you organize your plan of attack, here is a list. Check it every day. In fact, I recommend that you review the list in the morning to remind yourself of what needs to be done. Persistence is key. Your battle will not be won in a day or two, but you can achieve victory in a matter of weeks if you give it your full effort.

1. Stay motivated. Remind yourself how destructive the Worry Monster can be and how he is draining the happiness from your life. The more motivated you are, the more successful you will be in your quest to banish excessive anxiety from your thoughts. Although it may seem not as important

as other things you have scheduled that day, make NOT worrying a priority. Don't allow yourself to be lazy. Laziness is one of the prime reasons people fail to reach their goals. They're not incapable of persevering; they just lose focus and do something easier or more enjoyable.

2. To keep yourself on track, do a Worry Record each day. This will help you monitor your progress and determine your worry patterns. It will tell you what kinds of issues are most worrisome and how you react physically to your worry. Using the daily Worry Record, you will be able to objectively monitor your condition. Most important, taking this step (like taking any type of action) will change you from being a passive victim to becoming an architect of your happiness.

3. Each time you have an unusually troublesome worry, pin it down. Do an Individual Worry Episode Analysis: figure out what negative thoughts are bothering you and how to challenge and replace them using logic, reasoning, and evidence-gathering. If something is upsetting you, imagine the worst outcome and think about how you would cope with it. If the worry is still persistent, use the desensitization technique. This method is outlined in chapter seven.

4. Practice daily relaxation exercises such as muscle relaxation, calming self-talk, or diaphragm breathing. Staying calm and keeping your body relaxed are essential. The calmer you are, the less tendency you have to worry. Conversely, the more tense you are, the more worries you will have.

5. For daytime worries, learn to distract yourself. If you notice that you are preoccupied with the wor-

ries inside your head, change your focus to the external world. Look at your surroundings. Notice the sounds in the room or the bird conversations outside your window. Touch something on your desk, rub your armchair, or stroke your dog's fur. This is an easy way to derail the worry express.

6. Learn to laugh at yourself and your problems. Humor is a wonderful way of taking your worries less seriously. Just like the proverbial apple, humor will keep the psychiatrist away.

7. If you have been prescribed medication for your anxiety, take it exactly as indicated by your doctor. Try not to miss any doses. If you have a question, don't hesitate to call for clarification.

8. Don't be discouraged if you have a bad day. Instead of getting depressed and feeling defeated, think of it as a learning experience. Find out what you have been doing wrong, correct it, and go forward.

9. When you have a good day, compliment yourself. Give yourself the verbal equivalent of a big pat on the back.

10. Keep note of all the good things you do and all the successes you have — large or small. It is likely that you have been underestimating yourself for a long time. No matter how your life has gone up to this point, recognize that you — like all humans — have intrinsic worth.

11. Read items one to ten again.

The ability to live happily is within your grasp. With these strategies, you should be able to banish the Worry Monster from your life, never to return. Once you master these techniques, you will be able to apply them to all sorts of problems.

Martin E. Sodomsky, M.D.

Section Five
Resources

How to Find Help

Ideally, it is best to use this book along with the help of a mental health provider. Two heads are better than one when trying to defeat the Worry Monster.

If you decide to seek treatment, remember this: you must actively participate in the process. It will not do you any good to expect the therapist to do it all for you. To be successful, you must do your homework assignments, carry out the worry tracking described in this book, take notes, and become totally involved in the process. Numerous studies show that patients who actively participate in their treatment improve more quickly and get better results overall.

There are a number of ways to find professional help. You can ask friends who have undergone treatment or call acquaintances familiar with the mental health field in your area. You can look in the Yellow Pages under psychiatrist or psychologist. Before committing to a particular individual, ask how much experience he or she has in dealing with anxiety disorders. In addition, ask if they have experience in cognitive or behavioral psychotherapy, two types of approaches which are based in changing thoughts or behaviors. Psychiatrists or psychologists who specialize in psychodynamic or analytic therapy may not be the best choice to treat anxiety disorders. For these particular types of mental health problems, a cognitive or behavioral approach seems to be most effective.

When you have found someone with the right combination of expertise and therapy style, schedule an interview with them to see whether you are well-matched. If the therapist seems competent and you think you can work together, personality may not be so important. However, if you feel uncomfortable or take an instant dislike to the therapist, it might be wise to keep looking.

Another source of mental health providers is the Anxiety Disorders Association of America. You can learn more about the association by visiting its Web site at *http:// www.adaa.org/*. The site lists members by location and includes details about their particular fields of expertise.

If you have both generalized anxiety disorder and depression, you should find a psychiatrist or a psychologist with expertise in treating both of these conditions.

In some cases, people see a psychologist or a social worker (generally someone with a master's degree in social work) for psychotherapy, and a psychiatrist for medication. In other cases, patients may see a psychologist for therapy and receive medication from their primary care physician.

You may find the following books helpful:

1. *Master Your Panic and Take Back Your Life*, by Denise F. Beckfield, Ph.D. — a very thorough outline of how to deal with panic disorder.

2. *Mind Over Mood*, by Dennis Greenberger, Ph.D., and Christine A. Padesky, Ph.D. — discusses cognitive therapy and how to apply its principles to anxiety, depression, and anger.

3. *The Anxiety & Phobia Workbook*, by Edmund J. Borne, Ph.D. — a widely-used book with a great deal of information on relaxation training, breathing, assertiveness, and nutrition.

4. *The Laughter Prescription*, by Dr. Laurence J. Peter and Bill Dana — explains how to employ laughter in the healing process. Humor is very helpful for dealing with anxiety disorders.

5. *How to Stop People from Pushing Your Buttons*, by Albert Ellis, Ph.D., and Arthur Lange, Ed.D. Also *The Art of Rational Living*, by Albert Ellis, Ph.D., and Robert A. Harper, Ph.D.

6. *The Boy Who Couldn't Stop Washing*, by Judith L. Rapoport, M.D. — helpful for those with both GAD and OCD.

7. *Brain Lock*, by Jeffrey M. Schwartz, M.D. — another good book for the treatment of OCD.

8. *Getting Control*, by Leo Baer, Ph.D. — also good for OCD.

9. *Mastery of Your Specific Phobia*, by Martin M. Antony, Ph.D., Michelle G. Craske, Ph.D., and David H. Barlow, Ph.D. — addresses the treatment of phobias.

10. *The Feeling Good Handbook,* by David D. Burns, M.D. — a very good book for generalized anxiety disorder. Burns addresses communication issues and suggests ways to handle anxiety and depression.

11. *Dying of Embarrassment*, by Barbara G. Markway, Ph.D., et al — helpful for those with both GAD and social anxiety.
12. *Social Phobia*, by John R. Marshall, M.D. — gives good suggestions for overcoming social anxiety.
13. *Worry*, by Edward M. Hallowell, M.D.

Martin E. Sodomsky, M.D.

Section Six
The Worry Monster in Verse

Why Poetry?

Over the past 15 years, I have written poems as a hobby. I must confess that many times the ideas for these poems came to me early in the morning when I was still in my pajamas. I would quickly write the verses down on scraps of paper before my creative juices ran dry.

Most of the poems are fairly short and rather whimsical. I used them as a way to express the ideas of cognitive behavioral therapy in a somewhat light, concise and often humorous manner. I have shared many of the poems with my patients, who have found them both entertaining and helpful.

My wife convinced me to include these poems in the book. I went back and forth wondering if it was a good idea or not. Many in the publishing field told me not to do so. Finally, my wife said, "Just stop worrying and put them in."

So here they are. I hope you enjoy them.

The Worry Monster

Don't feed the Worry Monster,
His appetite is endless.
Juicy thoughts of disaster
He likes with romaine lettuce.

Never feed the Worry Monster,
He'll only ask for more.
Thoughts of bankruptcy and cancer
He especially adores.

Feed not the Worry Monster,
Don't share with him your wealth.
Don't let that shady character
Use up your time and health.

Don't feed the Worry Monster,
Starve him till he dies.
Then you'll be the master
Of your planet and your skies.

The Child Within

Let the child within you out to play,
Let him (her) have some fun.
Let him touch and feel the clay,
Let him dance and sing and run.

Let the child within you out of jail,
He's done nothing wrong.
Let him spin that fairy tale,
Let him know that he belongs.

Let the child within you take control
Of your life sometimes.
Your days then will feel more whole,
Your moments more sublime.

Let the child within you have more love
Kiss and hug him more.
Remind yourself what you're made of,
So go unlock the door.

Role Model

Stand tall like the saguaro,
Be tough like the prickly pear.
Your own path always follow —
What they think, do not care.

Travel like the roadrunner,
Seek adventure everywhere;
In the winter and the summer,
Care not how you compare.

Reach high like the century plant
And try and touch the sky;
Ignore those who say you can't—
Keep looking with a hopeful eye.

So let the desert show you
How in adversity to flourish;
The heat outside can't make you bow
When inside there is courage!

Problems

When you have some problems—
As sometimes you will—
And those darn problems
Just won't sit still.

So what can you do
About those pesky pests?
You have thought them through
Yet your mind simply won't rest.

One solution I have used—
In fact one of many—
You might be amused,
You might think it zany.

Just go up the stairs—
Go to the second floor—
And leave those rotten cares
Back on the first floor.

Then relaxed you will feel—
You can finally let go—
All those squeaky wheels
Reside safely below.

Regarding Change

I can't change the sun,
No matter how I try;
And I'd have no fun
If I tried to change the sky.

I can't change the rain
And can't change the snow;
I would try in vain
And have nothing to show.

I can't change the flowers
And can't change the trees;
And though I'd try for hours,
I can't change the bees.

I can't change you,
I'd ruin my health;
So I must conclude
I can only change myself.

Martin E. Sodomsky, M.D.

The New Columbus

The world then was not flat—
An astonishing discovery!
People had to change their facts
And change the way they see.

Yet even more surprising
One day you will find—
You'll be realizing,
It will blow your mind—

Facts you will uncover
On that glorious day!
You'll happily discover
That, after all, you are OK.

It's Good to Know

It's good to know
Those daily blues
Are not made of steel —
They are made of cobwebs
And you can sweep them away.

It's good to know
Those daily blahs
Are not made of lead —
They are made of dust
And you can blow them away.

It's good to know
Those daily downs
Are not made of concrete —
They are made of jelly
And you can wash them away.

It's good to know
Your daily foes
Are rather weak —
And you are very strong.

Enough's Enough

Stop being your fearful self—
That's not who you are.
Put your shyness on the shelf,
Polish up your star.

Stop being a scaredy-cat—
That's no way to be.
Confidence is where it's at,
That will set you free.

And better not apologize
For those things you do—
It's time that you recognize
You're a person too.

Put an end to hesitation—
You've done that far too long.
So substitute determination,
Exuberance and song.

Draw the curtain on anxiety—
That play is finally done.
Now it's time for you and me
To once again have fun.

Regarding Intimacy

Why are people
Afraid to be close—
Can't seem to ask
For what they want most?

Why do people
Avoid so much—
Avoid others' eyes,
Avoid others' touch?

Why is it people
Can be so blind
That love—though easy—
Is so hard to find?

A fear of rejection,
The probable cause.
Yet the time for affection
Is no time to pause.

The Director

Are you making a movie,
As so often you do,
And is that movie
Making you blue?

To me it would seem,
I say as a friend,
Change that last scene
So happy it ends.

Are you writing a song
With lyrics so sad;
And is that dreary song
Making you sad?

Well, compose a new song.
Why not create
A pleasant love song
That will make you feel great?

As artists we're free,
With new canvas each hour,
To draw a dead tree
Or a flaming red flower.

So why not today
Be one cheerful fellow;
So don't choose the gray,
Instead choose bright yellow!

Patience

No matter how severe the storm may be,
No matter how loud the thunder;
Though the wind blows forcefully,
You still need not surrender.

No matter how dark the day may be,
No matter how steady the rain;
Soon enough they will not be
And the sun will shine again.

And though the crisis be intense,
And so hard to endure;
Doctor time will soon dispense
The medicine, the cure.

Too Much Time

Too much time do I spend in the land of serious;
Too little time do I spend in the land of play.
And yet it is quite mysterious
I can choose how I spend my day.

But the reason I decide
Serious to be my daily goal—
The answer I cannot hide—
I like to be in control.

Uncertainty

Rarely does a day go by,
Now more than ever before,
That waves of uncertainty
Come upon my shore.

Some waves are very large,
Some are rather small;
But no matter what their size,
I despise them all.

I yearn for more certainty,
Then I could relax;
But as soon as I attain it,
Another wave attacks.

So what I must find,
I know I can afford;
Before I lose my mind,
A certainty-surfboard.

Movie Misery

Do you go to the movies too often—
The ones inside your head—
And do they make you feel just rotten
And fill your soul with dread?

Do you spend too much time at these movies—
Even though you have seen them before—
So your day is filled with misery
And your mind is full of horror?

You know there are no happy endings—
And no uplifting themes—
Fear, guilt and regretting
In scene after scene after scene.

Would you like to try an experiment?
Don't watch those movies today.
And if you want some real excitement,
Just go outside and play.

The Here and Now

When you have your mind
In the Here and Now,
There, peace you'll find;
Don't ask me how.

But when you give much thought
To those yesterdays,
Your stomach will knot
With guilt that stays.

Or when you focus too much
On those vague tomorrows,
Your body will clutch
To all imagined sorrows.

So may I humbly suggest—
And please don't resent—
To live life at its best,
Keep your eyes on the present.

Extreme Makeover

Do you take offense
At matters quite slight
With aggravation intense
That stays through the night?

Are you easily hurt
By an occasional neglect —
Your brain goes inert,
Your ego feels wrecked?

If your skin is so thin
To life's hard knocks,
Then the best way to win —
Get some emotional Botox.

The Voice of Gloom

That voice of gloom,
That sometimes speaks
With words of doom
Of goals unreached —

That voice of gloom
That makes you tense,
That darkens your room
With chilled suspense —

That voice so bad
You feel so stuck,
That voice so sad —
Is Donald Duck!

I hope my poems will prove useful to you. Remember,
ideas can be a powerful force in your life, leading to either
growth or despair. It's important that you choose your ideas
carefully, and, remember, don't feed the Worry Monster!

About the Authors

Martin E. Sodomsky, M.D., is a psychiatrist, currently residing in Tucson, Arizona, with his wife, Marilyn. He is a widely recognized expert in the treatment of anxiety disorders in the Tucson area.

Karen Wood is a freelance medical writer based in Tucson, Arizona.

Breinigsville, PA USA
09 December 2010
250944BV00002B/1/A